Mexican Memoir

A Personal Account of Anthropology and Radical Politics in Oaxaca

HOWARD CAMPBELL

BERGIN & GARVEY
Westport, Connecticut • London

Library of Congress Cataloging-in-Publication Data

Campbell, Howard, 1957–
    Mexican memoir : A personal account of anthropology and radical politics in
Oaxaca / Howard Campbell.
      p. cm.
    Includes bibliographical references and index.
    ISBN 0–89789–780–3 (alk. paper)—ISBN 0–89789–781–1 (pbk. : alk. paper)
    1. Zapotec Indians—Politics and government.   2. Zapotec Indians—Government
relations.   3. Zapotec Indians—Social conditions.   4. Ethnology—Mexico—Juchitán de
Zaragoza—Field work.   5. Political anthropology—Mexico—Juchitán de
Zaragoza.   6. Juchitán de Zaragoza (Mexico)—Ethnic relations.   7. Juchitán de
Zaragoza   (Mexico)—Politics and government.   8. Juchitán de Zaragoza
(Mexico)—Social conditions.
    F1221.Z3 C35   2001
    305.897′607274—dc21   00–048607

British Library Cataloguing in Publication Data is available.

Library of Congress Catalog Card Number: 00–048607
ISBN: 0–89789–780–3
        0–89789–781–1 (pbk.)

First published in 2001

Bergin & Garvey, 88 Post Road West, Westport, CT 06881
An imprint of Greenwood Publishing Group, Inc.
www.greenwood.com

Printed in the United States of America

The paper used in this book complies with the
Permanent Paper Standard issued by the National
Information Standards Organization (Z39.48–1984).

10 9 8 7 6 5 4 3 2 1

For Ruthie, Noela, and Vero

Contents

Photo essay follows page 74

Preface

Many people helped make possible my research in Oaxaca. I have tried to acknowledge all of them in my previous publications. Here I wish to thank those who read and made comments on drafts of this book. I especially thank David Kisela and Marc Thompson for their careful reading and many suggestions to improve grammar and style. John Monaghan, Les Field, and David Tavárez, all of whom are talented Latinamericanists, provided much helpful advice. Other patient and supportive readers included Steve Best, Sam Brunk, George Campbell, Howard E. Campbell, John Chance, Jeremy Cook, Héctor García, Eliza Holloway, Cheryl Howard, Karím Ley-Alarcón, Theresa May, Deborah Morgan, Rafael Nuñez, David Stemper, Flor Urías, Joshua Villalobos, Willam White, and one anonymous reviewer.

Introduction

This is an account of anthropological fieldwork on radical politics and cultural revivalism in southern Mexico. Memoirs or narrative ethnographies, such as this one, are usually associated with the rise of postmodern anthropology (Clifford and Marcus 1986; Behar 1993).[1] But this is not a postmodern ethnography, at least not in the sense of an ethnography devoted to textual experimentation, classless politics, or an ironic atittude (Tyler 1986, 1987; Clifford 1988; Marcus 1999; Best and Kellner 1997). The title has no implied double meaning or pun. Foucault, Baudrillard, and Derrida are not cited and I use few French words. Eschewing the utopian rhetoric that has become commonplace in some recent discussions of anthropology's present and future (e.g., Marcus 1998), this book provides an inside look at the people, places, emotions, and experiences that animated my fieldwork. In Gupta and Ferguson's (1997, 5) terms, this is "location-work."

In what follows I describe and analyze my interactions with Isthmus Zapotec people (and others) that occurred during my fieldwork conducted primarily in the 1980s in Oaxaca, Mexico. My research examined a "new social movement," COCEI,[2] that became one of the most successful grassroots political organizations in Latin America. In 1981, through an alliance with the Mexican Communist Party, COCEI won municipal elections in Juchitán, Oaxaca, which became the first city in Mexico to have a leftist government since the revolution (Campbell 1994). I also studied and worked with Zapotec intellectuals who fueled an influential indigenous cultural revival (Campbell et al. 1993). On a personal level, my anthropological career was furthered and complicated by marriage to an Isthmus Zapotec woman. The dissolution of the marriage near the end of my research raises serious questions about the relationships between anthropologists and "their people."

The book pivots around several dynamic tensions or contradictions that propelled my fieldwork. The central tension was my shifting relationship to Zapotec people that included participation in an extended family network, adoption of a Zapotec child and raising her in the United States, and confronting suspicion. However, I eventually engaged in numerous collaborations and friendships with Zapotec intellectuals and activists while studying COCEI. A second tension concerned my immersion in a largely male world of indigenous politicians and bohemian artists, in the context of a society known for its cult of women and mythical matriarchy. A third disjuncture involved research in "multiple sites" (Marcus 1998): primarily (a) on family dynamics, language, and customs in San Blas, Oaxaca,[3] and (b) ethnic politics, cultural revivalism, and gender relationships in Juchitán, Oaxaca. These issues are examined through a political economy perspective that, while critical of the "postmodern turn" in anthropology, adopts some of postmodernism's concepts and outlook (especially its emphasis on self-critical ethnographic writing, the rethinking of "rapport," and addressing the multisited nature of ethnography's subject).

Juchitán, the main site of my fieldwork, is located near the Chiapas border in southeastern Mexico on the Isthmus of Tehuantepec, a thin strip of land that separates the Pacific Ocean from the Gulf of Mexico (see map). The city of approximately 100,000 habitants is the commercial hub of the Isthmus and is located along the Pan-American highway and Trans-Isthmus highway that connects Veracruz and southern Oaxaca. Juchitán, once a peasant agricultural village, is today a busy, modern city, yet it retains much of its native character. Most Juchitecos are bilingual Zapotec Indians and the indigenous culture is visible in fiestas, women's colorful blouses and skirts, language, local cuisine, and the lifestyle and customs of the people. The Isthmus is a hot, tropical zone adjacent to the sparkling Pacific Ocean and muddy lagoons.

Isthmus of Tehuantepec

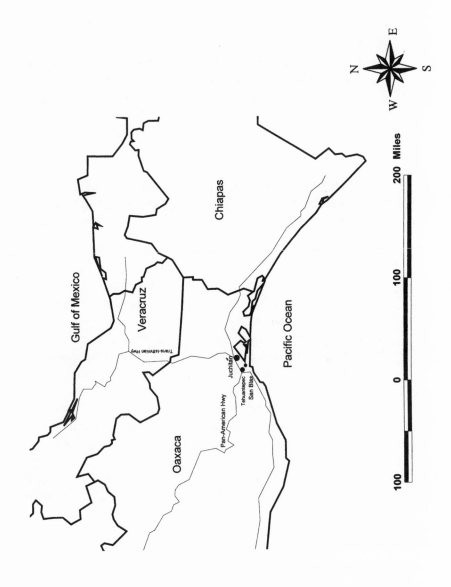

The huge Juchitán market is run by women, as are many local businesses. Zapotec men work in local commerce, schools, and government and also as fishermen, farmers, and laborers in the large oil
refinery twenty miles away in Salina Cruz. San Blas, a Zapotec peasant
village of about 20,000 people, is situated behind a hill that overlooks
the larger mestizo community of Tehuantepec. To some degree, San
Blas is a picture of what Juchitán was like fifty years ago. Almost all residents are Zapotec and fluent in the language. The life of the community is dominated by agricultural labor in the nearby corn and mango
fields and a never-ending round of colorful fiestas and religious processions. The rich Oaxacan community traditions and customs of San Blas
have not yet been overrun by modern technology and industrialism.[4]

POSTMODERNISM AND CONTEMPORARY
ETHNOGRAPHY: A CRITIQUE OF MARCUS AND
CLIFFORD AND A RATIONALE FOR THIS BOOK

The two foremost proponents of postmodernism in anthropology
are George Marcus and James Clifford (Clifford and Marcus 1986;
Clifford 1988). The postmodern approach to ethnography is
best-established in Marcus's book *Ethnography Through Thick and
Thin* (1998). According to Marcus's daunting agenda, future
ethnographies should be multisited, experimental, reflexive, and inter-
disciplinary. This means that anthropological studies should occur simultaneously in several places, engage in literary innovations,
comment on the anthropologists' role in the creation of the ethnography, and cross academic boundaries. Marcus's postmodern approach
directly attacks area studies ethnography and resistance-oriented subaltern studies. It advocates research on political elites and espouses
moral neutrality.

Postmodern critiques of single-site research, "objectivity,"
essentialized cultures,[5] and "rapport" were part of wide-ranging
changes in anthropology that emerged as ethnographers confronted
new theoretical problems and contexts of research in the 1980s and
1990s (Ortner 1999). Much of this has been laudable, especially the attempt to renovate research through greater attention to the textual and
political contexts of ethnography, and the fragmented character of culture in the modern world (Marcus 1999). Ethnography undoubtedly
must be transformed to meet the needs of changing times and peoples,
and postmodernism will surely play a key role in that process. Nonethe-

less, there are elements of the postmodern agenda that I consider politically problematic and to which the present book stands in contradistinction (cf. Best 1995).

The present fieldwork account, while incorporating aspects of the postmodern critique, is much more modest. It is a memoir about life in Oaxaca with a distinctive political position; I openly support the COCEI movement I studied. While advocating politicized ethnography, however, the book is also critical of "political correctness,"[6] but from the left not the right.

Unlike many postmodernists, I feel that there is still a need in anthropology for ethnographic work focused on peoples located primarily within particular areas such as the Isthmus of Tehuantepec (notwithstanding globalism), and for an activist anthropology that takes sides and that, despite moral ambiguities, supports one group against another. Furthermore, I believe that collaboration with "informants" is possible and preferable to the gloomy "complicity" that Marcus (1998) proposes as a substitute for the quintessential ethnographic relationship that we used to call rapport.

Rabinow (1986), Clifford (1988), Fischer (1999), and other innovators of postmodern anthropology call for a new kind of anthropological study that is redesigned to cope with emerging subjectivities and phenomena, that is worldwide in scope, and eclectic in its use of ideas and theories. While I agree with these points, I am concerned about the tepid, apolitical, or even elitist orientation of much of postmodern anthropology (Ahmed and Shore 1995; Hubinger 1996).[7] Should we follow Marcus's advice (1998, 20) to emphasize "moral ambiguities" and avoid "filiation to just one group of subjects among whom fieldwork is done"? Is the commitment to a group of people in a particular place an anachronism in a transcultural world?

Because of my particular political orientation, I decided not to give equal time in my ethnographic account to members of the PRI,[8] Mexico's governing party for seventy-one years.[9] In my research, I defended the COCEI (composed primarily of Zapotec farmers, market women, and workers) instead of placing myself "between groups in direct . . . opposition" (Marcus 1998, 20). This outlook prevented me from seeing the innovative contribution of postmodern ethnography that Marcus claims is exemplified in Santiago Villaveces-Izquierdo's dissertation on Colombian elite responses to violence (Marcus 1998, 21–25).[10]

Instead of focusing on "the perpetrators, victims, or actual acts of violence themselves and their immediate consequences" (Marcus 1998, 22), Villaveces-Izquierdo studied the "Colombian middle- and upper-middle class culture of fear and indifference" and the "responses of the elites to violence" (23). Villaveces-Izquierdo's main site of fieldwork was the Colombian Constitutional Court and he relied on experts on violence known as violentologists. His main informant was a "highly reputed psychoanalyst." So much for the preferential option for the poor that has long motivated Latin American Studies.

No doubt Villaveces-Izquierdo's work will produce interesting results. However, what concerns me about this research, and the postmodern intellectual project it embodies, is that it is explicitly designed to take the place of "traditional" research on the poor and subaltern (Ahmed and Shore 1995). Elite actors substitute for the peasants and workers who previously peopled ethnographies of Latin America. Painful social realities are discarded as ethnographic subject matter in favor of the investigation of discourse. According to Marcus (1998, 85–86), the anthropological resistance literature, allied with particular social movements and people, is dead. What would Subcomandante Marcos and the Zapatistas in the jungles of Chiapas or the *coceísta* radicals in Juchitán think of this?

Similar choices face the budding ethnographers of the United States–Mexico border where I live. In Ciudad Juárez, Chihuahua, international drug trafficking has become the largest business in town. Each year hundreds of people die as a result of drug violence. At the same time, a thriving narco-culture has invaded the streets, dance halls, and radio airwaves of the region. Should aspiring anthropologists focus on the drug trade itself, which now employs literally thousands of people in the El Paso/Juárez area, or should they concentrate on the "narco-style" espoused in the hundreds of narco-corridos that are the most visible symbols of a narco discourse? Clearly, we need both kinds of research. It seems that Villaveces-Santiago and other postmodernists favor the discourse-oriented approach, but in these particular cases, at least, the more challenging and innovative work would be to research the violence and drug businesses directly.

There are many other examples in my home region that illustrate this point. In addition to the drug-trafficking plague, Ciudad Juárez has suffered the killing (often accompanied by rape) of at least 200 women since 1993. Should local research focus on the victims, their families, and the perpetrators, or would more stylish work examine the government and media's representations of the murders? What about undocumented immigration—should the hip anthropologist live with and study Mexican "illegal" immigrants or would it be more experimental to deconstruct the INS's (Immigration and Naturalization Service, "*la migra*") discourse about "illegal aliens"? In my ethnography, I chose to investigate a radical Indian peasant movement and its ideology instead of the ways in which local elites and the dominant PRI party viewed the movement (i.e., as barbaric) and the strategies they took to contain it. Should I have created space for the voices of those who have always dominated the Mexican national and regional media? Should I have given elites a chance?

How easily many postmodernists discard the "old" left political and scholarly agenda (Best and Kellner 1991). Yet they seem to have replaced it with a kind of ethnographic account that fetishizes the literary text and emphasizes style over substance (Moore 1996). According to Marcus, the value of an ethnography, today, is measured by "the aesthetics of argument, their moral power, and their manner of achieving these . . . a certain art world-like practice of critique and assessment of individual works has substituted for an older style of sustained assessment of shared objects of study" (1998, 242). Is ethnography just another style or fashion? Will we be forever plagued by ethnographies with cute, polysemic titles? Must postmodern irony rule the day? Perhaps, in the long run, good basic ethnographic writing will be more enduring to readers than arcane, avant-garde, experimental texts.

I also question if we should settle for Marcus's "complicity" in place of rapport. Is productive collaboration impossible? If "complicity" is the agenda, then what matters is with whom we are "complicit." Marcus (1998) chooses to be complicit with the Tonga elite and wealthy Americans. In *Ethnography Through Thick and Thin*, he celebrates his complicity with the Getty Trust, Reaganite Cold Warriors, and the Institute for Advanced Study.[11] With friends like these, why waste time with working people or farmers? Marcus's elite-centered vision also leads him to declare (by fiat) the death of subaltern studies and the inadequacy of Marxist political economy. Additionally, he calls for the subordination of resistance studies (85). For Marcus, postmodern culture is classless (50), so why focus on the downtrodden? The strangest aspect of this argument is Marcus's gleeful invocation of "partnership in an evil action" through "complicit" fieldwork (124).

Other contributors to the rethinking of anthropology have been more effective in exposing ways in which the mere possibility of doing anthropology has been predicated on colonial or neocolonial relationships (Rosaldo 1989). In this sense, fieldwork historically was made possible by political and economic realities that the fiction of rapport elided. Marcus (1998) asks ethnographers to face up to this history of inequality and acknowledge their involvement in structures of power and privilege. I agree. But why not seek constructive collaboration with one's "subjects" of study and attempt to redress or attenuate the structures of unequal power that historically have governed ethnographic work? Marcus discards collaboration as an effective ethnographic option because, he says, it reinforces the traditional mise-en-scène of fieldwork and sustains the representation of "bounded cultures." I question whether this must be the case. Could there not be a collaboration that is sensitive to the complexities of postmodern culture, and acknowledges the problems of colonialism but fights against them?[12] Even if collaborations are not fool-proof, I feel that we should make cooperation with our research "subjects" a high priority.[13] Examples of such collaborations are illustrated in this book.

Postmodern anthropology clashes with other issues fundamental to my research in the Isthmus of Tehuantepec, namely, love of the land, community, and one's "bounded" culture. Marcus argues for a "break with the trope of community," an end to a focus on ethnic groups rooted in a particular place and studies of single cultures with distinct boundaries. What does this mean for Amerindian beliefs and practices that encourage nature worship, not in the abstract, not in relationship to some shifting postmodern landscape, but of a specific piece of ground? In an age of rampant ecological destruction—of, for example, the Chimalapas jungle and the stunning Pacific beaches along the Oaxaca coast—should we support thinking that suggests individual places do not matter, that the local (and local knowledge) is passé?[14]

Community is not just a trope. Try telling a Juchiteco that what matters is not his particular people and locality (Juchitán) but the multiple sites in which he operates. His reply might be that, no, "*Juchitán es el ombligo del mundo*" ("Juchitán is the center of the world," literally "the world's navel"), because that is where his *xquipi*[15] (placenta) is buried.[16] I think there is still space in anthropology and contemporary culture for the premodern, the "primitive," the obsessive love of specific places and peoples. This feeling was expressed to me by one of my informants who said that Zapotecs worshipped trees, but not in the abstract, and he pointed to an old, gnarled *biadxi* (plum tree) in Cheguigo where the *vela biadxi* (plum tree festival) is held each year. Zapotecs call themselves the "cloud people" (those who came down to earth from the clouds) and their culture developed in villages and city-states with a high degree of endogamy and distinctiveness from neighboring communities. Many of these towns were prototypes of Wolf's closed corporate community model and are hundreds, even thousands, of years old. Of course they are affected by globalization and transcultural processes. But their rootedness is a reality that the multisited, postmodern approach may overlook. Defending a given piece of land and culture—as in the Juchitán case—may require a strategic essentialism that goes against the grain of trendy postmodernity. Postmodernism may breathe new life into the local, it may also destroy it (Best and Kellner 1997, 14).[17]

James Clifford, Marcus's coeditor of the path-breaking *Writing Culture* volume (1986), is the other leading exponent of postmodernism in anthropology. Clifford's 1997 book, *Routes*, develops his notion of ethnography as a form of travelling. Postmodernity, for Clifford, is the "new world order of mobility, of rootless histories" (1). From this standpoint, "everyone's on the move" and dwelling itself is a form of travel (2). Clifford describes travel as "an increasingly complex range of experiences: practices of crossing and interaction that troubled the localism of many assumptions about culture" (3). Anthropological fieldwork emerges from this analysis as "a series of travel encounters" (2).

While altering the mise-en-scène of traditional fieldwork, now conceived as contact zone or travel encounter, Clifford leaves room for an ethnographic account, such as this one, that emphasizes subaltern identities, social movements, and "indigenous resistance." Like Marcus, Clifford signals the end of the fieldwork relationship known as rapport. Unlike Marcus, Clifford sees hope for an informant/anthropologist "alliance," instead of the dreary "complicity" (1997, 41). The new subjects of ethnographies, then, will be "hybrid 'natives'," travellers like the anthropologist through postmodern cultural terrain. What is important in this hybridity, according to Clifford, is "politically . . . who deploys nationality or transnationality, authenticity or hybridity, against whom, with what relative power and ability to sustain a hegemony" (10).

This important observation brings politics back into the postmodern picture, where Marcus had seen a classless situation. As Clifford rightly notes, who is able to travel—in some cases men rather than women—is a matter of power and privilege or, in other cases, coercion. The main problem I see in Clifford's approach is that its euphoria for culture as travel sweeps away still vital cultural processes of rootedness, histories, and homelands (cf. Mintz 2000, 176). Culture is always, in some sense, in motion, and travel is especially important today. But not all cultures move as quickly or are as obsessed with newness and change as that of North America. Could the U.S. experience of continuous immigration and relentless cultural change have colored Clifford's view of global cultural processes? Surely contemporary Chinese or Iraqis (heirs to approximately 10,000 years of history, however contested) or Zapotecs view "dwelling" somewhat differently. Not all cultures are "on the road," all the time.

However, most of Clifford's meditations on contemporary anthropology are insightful, especially his discussion of changing notions of "the field" and the fieldworker's relationship to it. Clifford argues that definitions of the field "are changing, as the geography of distance and difference alters in postcolonial/neocolonial situations, as power relations of research are reconfigured, as new technologies of transport and communication are deployed, and as 'natives' are recognized for their specific worldly experiences and histories of dwelling and traveling" (1997, 58). He contends that the idea of "fieldwork-as-dwelling" (67) has been decentered or interrupted, though it remains an important part of many anthropologists' disciplinary identity, including mine.

In my case, one of my most important informants was my wife, who continually provided me with information about Zapotec ways of life, whether we were in Oaxaca, Mexico City, the United States, or Europe. Later, one of my key informants lived with me in El Paso, Texas, for several years, and we engaged in an ongoing dialogue about Zapotec people. Other key interactions and interviews occurred in Mexico City and Tucson, Arizona. Thus, important aspects of my fieldwork took place outside the Isthmus of Tehuantepec, the homeland of the Isthmus Zapotecs and the COCEI political movement, although the Isthmus was definitely the principal location of my research.

Although my previous research was critical of some aspects of COCEI's ideology and tactics, on the whole I was supportive of the movement because I think it represented the most progressive political and social movement in the Isthmus, and one of the most positive indigenous organizations in Mexico. My marriage to a Zapotec woman no doubt influenced my political commitments although it did not bias me in favor of COCEI; many of her relatives are *priístas*, or hostile to the leftist movement. Whereas Marcus (1998, 74–75) downplays the issue of power and partisanship in ethnographic accounts and is "not interested in the cultural studies cliché of resistance by often sentimentalized 'Others' " (1998, 205), my fieldwork and writing were politically engaged.

Clifford, commenting on "ethnography's political dimensions," observes that "There are no guaranteed or morally unassailable [political] positions" (1997, 87). But political or moral complexity is no excuse for neutrality or inaction. If anthropology historically has been aided (and abetted) by colonialism and neocolonialism, the least we can do is support our research "subjects" in their struggles against it. Frankly, I am tired of the postmodern ironic attitude and the depoliticizing, immobilizing postmodern paradigms that have become so popular in anthropology and elsewhere (Ahmed and Shore 1995). Passion for a political cause or group of people (or an individual) may be fraught with peril but, as Sartre observed, there is no exit. Not to take sides is also a moral, ethical, and political decision. The key, as noted above, is with whom we choose to collaborate or build alliances.

My collaboration with Zapotec politicians and intellectuals consisted of articles, books, newspaper stories, and letters to the editor defending COCEI against the PRI and publicizing the movement's cause in outside media (e.g., Campbell 1990, 1993, 1996). Other lesser contributions to the COCEI organization included the donation of a typewriter and miscellaneous gifts to *coceísta* friends. I consider my friendships with numerous *coceístas* important, and not simply a means to an academic end.

Most anthropologists recognize that the "personal is political," but the personal is also critical because this is the area in which we may have the greatest impact on the people we study. Despite our often lofty goals and high-sounding rhetoric, anthropology is not usually very important in terms of the "big picture." The forces of world economic power and the political powers-that-be in most countries seldom consider anthropology. This is unfortunate, but it is unlikely to change in the near future. However, our personal interactions "in the field" have powerful impacts on people's lives and they matter.

My alliances with Zapotec painters, poets, and musicians (whom I refer to generically as "intellectuals") were also of an amicable nature. We spent time interacting in their homes and mine (including in El Paso) and at demonstrations, fiestas, parties, art studios, restaurants, marketplaces, and in the streets. The bars and the *Casa de la Cultura* (Cultural Center) of Juchitán were other important "contact zones." Our collaborations entailed several joint publications in the United States; bringing numerous Zapotec artists, musicians, and scholars to my home university, the University of Texas at El Paso (UTEP) for conferences and exhibits; establishing a Zapotec cultural event at UTEP; donating the royalties of *Zapotec Struggles* (Campbell et al. 1993) to a Oaxacan cultural organization; and being an editor of a Zapotec magazine.[18] Many of these collaborative efforts were initiated by Zapotec intellectuals. Above all, many Zapotec writers and painters have become my lifelong colleagues and future collaborators on cultural projects.

Marcus rightly notes the "powerful motivation of personal connection in shaping ethnography" (1998, 14). In my case, marriage to a Zapotec woman (Obdulia Campbell), whom I met in Mexico City, preceded my fieldwork in the Isthmus. She contributed to my research in ways too numerous to mention. From the time of our marriage in 1981 to the present we have engaged in discussions about Zapotec lifeways and language. Her influence on my thinking has been profound and multifaceted, although she did not accompany me during most of my Juchitán fieldwork in 1987–1988. In 1994 I adopted Obdulia's niece, her sister's daughter, which further strengthened my ties to the Isthmus Zapotec community. For these reasons, my research was always affected by personal factors. In "the field" I was recognized as having married a local woman whose family I lived with; hence I was less an outsider than the average anthropologist who passed through the region.

Given these circumstances, and that I was studying an idealistic, radical political movement with which I felt sympathy, I could not claim neutrality nor would I want to. My passion for my subject matter and the people I studied and collaborated with was considerable. It was the farthest thing imaginable from the kind of bloodless, detached postmodern irony that became popular in anthropology in the 1990s. When I was divorced from my wife in 1999 I began to feel that I no longer had a right to do research in the Isthmus. Eventually, Zapotec friends changed my thinking about this, and I recently returned to my old ethnographic haunts. Clearly, personal ties created through ethnography can be deep and intense and should not be taken lightly.

Marcus says that ethnography should not be about or allied with "bounded" cultural groups (1998, 20). This conflicts directly with my approach to ethnography. While well intentioned, his approach could lead to an insipid anthropology that is globalized, mobile, and fragmented—something like MTV, clever and shallow. Emotion and passionate commitment to specific people and places have been important elements of anthropology from the time of Mead to Rosaldo (1980). There is no reason why this should not continue despite the fast and fragmenting pace of global, transcultural processes.

This book is as much about me, the ethnographer, as it is about COCEI politicians and Isthmus Zapotec intellectuals. As many recent observers (Geertz 1988; Clifford 1988, 1997) have shown, "self-analysis" is often an essential part of contemporary ethnographies. My intention, however, is not to exalt my story, but to contribute to an anthropology in postmodern times that is self-critical, collaborative, politically progressive, and grounded in solid fieldwork.

OUTLINE OF CHAPTERS

Chapter 1 examines my initial encounters with Zapotecs, especially my ex-wife and her family. It also discusses my decision to research the Zapotec COCEI political movement and my passionate involvement with people and life in the Isthmus of Tehuantepec. In chapter 2, I focus on the main sites of my fieldwork in Juchitán, particularly COCEI political gatherings, bohemian cantinas, and fiestas. I also describe Isthmus people, places, and incidents that shaped my research experience. Another theme of the chapter is my rethinking of the U.S. political attitudes I learned as an anthropology graduate student and the ironies of being a male researcher exposed to the patriarchal side of a supposedly matriarchal society.

Chapter 3 examines Zapotec family life and customs in San Blas, Oaxaca. I discuss the beauty and richness of local customs and the physical environment as well as the ways in which the Isthmus Zapotec way of life is being transformed by national and international economic and cultural developments. Instead of celebrating emerging cultural hybridity, as is common among postmodern analysts, I lament cultural and ecological destruction in the Isthmus of Tehuantepec.

Chapter 4 describes my interactions with Zapotec politicians and evolving alliances with the COCEI movement. I consider the dilemmas of researching radical politics in a polarized environment and my growing friendships with *coceístas* and partisan commitment to their organization.

Chapter 5 explores the bohemian Zapotec art and intellectual scene including some of the major Juchiteco writers and painters, their milieu, and their key works. It also describes several projects on which we collaborated. While my relationships with luminaries of the Zapotec intellectual world were not always smooth, they did lead to more productive collaborations than were possible with the COCEI politicians.

Chapter 6 concludes the recounting of my main period of fieldwork and discusses my changing relationship to Zapotec people and "the field." I reflect on the consequences of passionate commitment to individuals and groups in fieldwork and the relevance of such ethnographic relationships to contemporary anthropology.

The epilogue describes a recent ethnographic visit to Juchitán and the challenges it posed to me as a person and anthropologist.

NOTES

1. The emergence of postmodern culture has been described by Best and Kellner (1991, ix) as the result of "a series of socioeconomic and cultural transformations in the 1970s and 1980s. . . . An explosion of media, computers and new technologies, a restructuring of capitalism, political shifts and upheavals, novel cultural forms, and new experiences of space and time produced a sense that dramatic developments have occurred throughout culture and society." These authors state that postmodern theory is found in "the writings of Michel Foucault, Gilles Deleuze and Felix Guattari, Jean Baudrillard, Jean-Francois Lyotard, Fredric Jameson, Ernesto LaClau, Chantal Mouffe, and others [who] articulate new perspectives that map the allegedly novel postmodern sociocultural conditions and develop new modes of theorizing, writing, subjectivity, and politics" (ix).

2. The Coalición Obrera Campesina Estudiantil del Istmo, Worker-Peasant-Student Coalition of the Isthmus of Tehuantepec, was founded in Juchitán, Oaxaca in 1973. COCEI has won mayoral elections in Juchitán four times and also elected numerous state and federal deputies and even senators. (This is a rare achievement for indigenous people in Mexico.) Its followers are called *coceístas*.

3. The town of San Blas is also known as San Blas Atempa.

4. At least this was the case at the time of my fieldwork. Today, San Blas residents are also being pulled in large numbers into the industrial economy dominated by PEMEX, the Mexican national oil company.

5. Essentializing or essentialism refers to an anthropological approach that treats cultures as unchanging, timeless entities with permanent, core characteristics that differentiate them from other cultures.

6. By "political correctness" I refer to a dogmatic political style, especially common in U.S. academia in the 1980s, that insisted on the rigid use of particular words and the adoption of specific supposedly "progressive" political positions. Normally, the term "political correctness" is used by the U.S. right to attack the left. While my political allegiance is to the left (broadly defined as a kind of Marxist, feminist, and anti-racist politics), I feel that the superficiality, doctrinality, and humorless character of leftist "political correctness" in the 1980s was harmful to the development of enduring critical ideas and social change.

7. For example, Marcus's recent pronouncements about ethnography seem like elite discourse meant for "the most noted anthropologists" and "senior and established scholars" working in the "major graduate programs" and "major departments" (1998, 231–253). Am I reading too much into this or is Marcus' constant invocation of "prominent research careers," the "most distinguished anthropologists" and the "senior generation" reflective of an elitist, conservative political agenda? Does the fact that Marcus studies elites (in Tonga and the United States) have to do with his call for an end to "commitment to some external movement" (1998, 244)?

8. PRI stands for the *Partido Revolucionario Institucional*, the Institutional Revolutionary Party. Its followers are called *priístas*.

9. Until the 2000 presidential elections, which occurred just as I finished this book, PRI was the world's longest ruling political party.

10. In addition to not appreciating the "striking . . . originality" (Marcus 1998, 28) of Villaveces-Izquierdo's dissertation, I find his claim bizarre that while many fieldworkers have a "muse" (i.e., key informant), "he or she is located off the map of the work (perhaps evident only in the Acknowledgements)." It is my impression that most researchers have a "muse" and that they usually locate that person in the center of their ethnographies.

11. In another part of the book, Marcus (1998, 105–131) describes "complicit" research on fascists and Nazis as exemplary!

12. Despite Marcus's claim that "complicit" ethnography is superior to collaboration, all of the studies he considers exemplary are authored by anthropologists (usually Western or Westernized anthropologists) without shared authority, at least as formal authors, by the subjects of study (1998, 105–131). In that sense, complicity does not seem an improvement over the traditonal "rapport." Authorial collaboration between ethnographer and "subject" is preferable.

13. Marcus's perspective also neglects indigenous anthropologists whose potential to create working collaborations with informants may be greater than that of the nonnative.

14. Ecological damage is directly linked with the destruction of local cultures. See Ostler (1999) for a discussion of the decline of linguistic diversity and its negative consequences for world culture.

15. A traditional Isthmus Zapotec practice is to bury the placenta of a newborn under the house. The average Istmeño plans to be buried in the cemetery next to their relatives. In this worldview, locality is primary.

16. This century Isthmus Zapotecs have migrated for work and educational opportunities primarily to Chiapas, Veracruz, Oaxaca City, and Mexico City. This migration, however, usually did not sever people's strong ties to the Isthmus. Unlike many parts of Oaxaca, people from Juchitán have seldom migrated to the United States to work in agriculture or other occupations.

17. Marcus' other ethnographic hobby horse that deserves some mention here is textual experimentation. For Marcus, the only good ethnography is an innovative and avant-garde one. That anthropologists are usually not literary virtuosos is well known. Indeed, textual experimentation in the wrong hands can be disastrous. In an era of declining sales of anthropology books we should consider moves to make ethnographies more pleasurable and accessible to the reader (cf. Mintz 2000, 177). I hope this is the case with this book. Two excellent and readable ethnographic works are Rabinow's *Reflections on Fieldwork in Morocco* (1977) and Bourgois's *In Search of Respect* (1995), neither of which is exotically innovative. Both get the job done.

18. Other collaborative efforts included selling paintings, donating art supplies, and donating dozens of books and articles to individuals and the Juchitán Cultural Center.

CHAPTER 1

An Anthropologist in the Isthmus of Tehuantepec

The first time I saw Tehuantepec it was not as an anthropologist but as a prospective groom. I remember arriving at the Isthmus in the morning exhausted from the twelve-hour ride from Mexico City and the diesel fumes and engine noises that spewed from the back of the bus. I vividly recall the orange tile roofs and white-washed colonial buildings in the center of town. Soon Obdulia, my future wife, and I were on our way to San Blas in a run-down taxi. As always in the region, it was hot and sticky. I was also steaming with tension as the taxi bounced its way through the dusty streets to San Blas, the Indian town tucked behind Jaguar Hill.

At that time, in the spring of 1981, San Blas had but one poorly paved street, but it was a big town whose red brick and white-washed cement block houses were tightly packed together along the narrow roads and alleys. We pulled up to 25 Hidalgo Street, a plain brick house whose green paint was flaking off. The main entrance to the home was a long, narrow cement hall, the *zaguán*. We walked into the house and I heard the loud shouting and laughing of a group of men. I was taken into the dark kitchen past the banana tree and flowers growing in the open, unroofed patio. I met my future mother-in-law, a stocky, jovial woman with long black hair and a brilliantly colored Tehuana *huipil* and billowy skirt. After a prudent wait I embarrassedly introduced my-self to Mr. Ruiz and in broken Spanish asked for his daughter's hand in marriage. I felt totally inadequate in this setting. My Spanish was weak, my Zapotec nonexistent, and I felt exhausted from the tropical weather and the newness of my surroundings. The jovial back-slapping and carousing of my future father-in-law and his drinking buddies (including two of my future brothers-in-law) did not offer comfort. I did not feel like celebrating. I wanted to go to a corner and hide.

Unfortunately, this was not an option, since the *zaguán* door was always open and a steady stream of neighbors, relatives, and curious onlookers continually came into the house to inspect the strange gringo who had come to marry a local. Dozens of people came to see me. Not just to glimpse, but to stare and even to pull on the hair of my arms that were a golden color they found exotic. I was amazed at how uninhibited the people were, and they seemed to have nothing to do but sit around and talk and joke endlessly. It seemed that I was the brunt of a joke. I could not even kill the anxiety with a few drinks because at that time I was on a vegetarian health kick and abstained from alcohol. The family food was greasy, heavily spiced, and emphasized meat—all of which were problems for me at the time. The water—dipped with a communal gourd out of a clay pot perched on a pedestal—was of questionable purity. The whole experience was overwhelming.

Perhaps the worst of it was the timelessness. The main activity in the house was sitting around in a group making meaningless (or so I thought) conversation. I wanted to go off by myself and read a book. I wished to return to Mexico City and escape this scene. At the time, the picturesque texture of local life was too much for me. I was still getting used to the idiosyncrasies of Mexican national culture. To be thrust into this indigenous environment was too much to handle at first. At the time, my knowledge of anthropology was limited and I had not built up the resistance to the heat and local bacteria that would later allow me to conduct successful fieldwork. The intense sociability of the people, their raucous humor, and the bohemian drinking bouts that I later cherished were then foreign to me. The communal customs, complex social networks, and simple beauty of daily life in San Blas were things that I would learn about and enjoy in the future.

As the July wedding date approached, Obdulia and I returned to Mexico City and made preparations, including inviting our urban friends and purchasing huge bunches of colorful gladiolas from the Sonora Market. We transported the flowers by taxi from the market to our apartment and then again by taxi to Mexico City's southern bus terminal (known as the TAPO). The packages of flowers weighed at least sixty pounds each and were difficult to carry. At one point I needed a rest from carrying them and set them upside down on the sidewalk. This was a mistake because I smashed some of the flower buds. In any event, most of the fragrant white flowers survived the trip to the Isthmus and beautifully adorned the ancient Santo Domingo Cathedral for the wedding ceremony in Tehuantepec. As I left the house for the wedding dressed in the obligatory dark slacks, black dress shoes and white *guayabera* (shirt), I still felt out of place, a feeling heightened by my father-in-law's scolding me for carrying a long comb that stuck out of my back pocket. Obdulia wore a stunning white wedding dress sewn by a *muxe'* (gay) tailor who flirted with me when we went to pick it up.

We were joined at the church by a large crowd of relatives and friends. The female guests were dressed in Zapotec *trajes,* the brightly colored, embroidered blouses and skirts that are an ethnic uniform for Isthmus women. The colonial church was redolent with the aroma of our expensive Mexico City gladiolas and spicy copal incense. The only modern touch in the proceedings was the use of a microphone by the slim, professional young priest. My nerves were on fire with apprehension at being the center of attention in a series of wedding rites and rituals that I only vaguely understood. But it was satisfying to feel the warm hugs of the *padrinos* (godparents) and relatives near the end of the ceremony. My pictures of the event record a tall, thin gringo towering over his shapely, dark-skinned bride. Other photos show us surrounded by grizzled, peasant grandparents wearing their finest dress clothes that, in the case of grandpa Anacleto, included his best pair of huaraches.

The end of the wedding was a relief, but this was only the beginning of the night's events. We had scheduled the wedding and reception for a Saturday night to avoid the long hours of bacchanalian drinking that accompany a morning wedding in the Isthmus. Our reasoning was that more people would tire and leave a nighttime event sooner than an all-day affair. This was a sensible approach, given that we were (that is, I was) responsible for feeding, and especially providing beer and liquor for, the hundreds of invited guests and party-crashing Blaseños.[1]

From the cathedral we walked, accompanied by the relatives and guests, in a long, winding procession through the old Tehuantepec plaza, up the dirt road and through the path carved through huge boulders that form the entrance to San Blas. It must have been quite a sight to the predominantly mestizo Tehuanos[2]: a huge crowd of Zapotecs following the lead of a skinny gringo in a wedding procession into the heart of the peasant Indian town that non-Indians feared and disparaged. When we reached the Ruiz family home, exhausted from the mile-long walk, we were greeted by the lively sounds of electric guitars of the wedding band and the glowing light bulbs that had been strung along the white walls of the surrounding houses. Narrow Hidalgo Street was filled on each side with hundreds of invited guests and hangers-on seated on metal folding chairs. At one end of the street sat the white three-layered wedding cake with ornaments depicting a huge bride and a diminutive groom in playful inversion of the real couple and reflecting the supposedly matriarchal culture of the Zapotecs.

The night's events are now a blur in my mind because most of the evening I served plates of *lomo huini* (a kind of spicy beef stew akin to the *chile colorado* eaten in the Southwest U.S.), cake, and cold beers to the guests; I accepted gifts and gave thanks, and generally exchanged chit-chat with the dozens of new in-laws whose names and importance in the family labyrinth I could not fully comprehend. I also danced the obligatory waltzes with Obdulia, our *madrina*,[3] and various other female relatives. I felt awkward as the focus of the stares of the crowd in the spotlighted center of the party. But I did my best to participate correctly in the dances and rites. I even collected more money from the guests than Obdulia in the *mediu xhiga* custom where the wedding guests dance up to the bride and groom and place money in brightly painted half-gourds that the new spouses hold in their laps. I eventually relaxed after drinking a few beers and dancing clumsily to the traditional wedding songs. I certainly amused the guests, whether because of my dancing prowess (unlikely) or because of the absurd sight of the lanky white boy trying to keep up with the fluid movements of the robust but elegant Istmeñas as they twirled to the waltzes, *sones*, and *musica tropical* (genres of Latin American popular music).

At about midnight, Obdulia and I quietly disappeared in a Volkswagen driven by our Mexico City friends. We left the multitude of celebrants raucously dancing and drinking to the music of the band. We left to avoid the traditional Isthmus custom in which the bride and groom supposedly have sex for the first time on their wedding night and then produce a white sheet with red blood on it, the "proof of virginity," which they proudly display to the crowd. This leads to the singing of *behua xhiña*, the red snapper song that celebrates blood, sex, and fertility. We spent the night at the Hotel Tehuantepec, a run-down tropical hotel, too tired to consummate the event, just wanting to get some sleep in the ferocious humid Isthmus night as mosquitoes buzzed out-side our window and the ceiling fan swooped overhead.

On our way to Cancún for our honeymoon we stopped for breakfast in Juchitán, Oaxaca. Juchitán! Even today the name causes chills to run down my spine. Juchitán, the Town of Women. The People's Govern-ment of Juchitán. Viva Juchitán Libre! Indigenous Utopia. Zapotec Cultural Renaissance. Gay Paradise. All of these images came to mind later when I knew more about the place. Since precolonial times, the Isthmus has been coveted by outsiders. The Aztecs, Spanish, French. Brasseur de Bourbourg, a French abbot, wrote a colorful travelogue about the exotic native peoples and customs. The Mexican radical in-telligentsia flocked to the Isthmus—Covarrubias's "Mexico South"—in the 1920s and 1930s. Diego Rivera caricatured Zapotec fi-estas and Frida Kahlo depicted herself as a Tehuana Amazon in numer-ous paintings. Edward Weston, Langston Hughes, Tina Modotti, Eisenstein, all came to the Isthmus . . . the list goes on and on (Camp-bell and Green 1996).

Juchitán once again became a cause célèbre in the 1980s when the radical COCEI's *Ayuntamiento Popular* (People's Government) was ousted from power and *coceísta* political prisoners became poster boys for the Mexican left. Juchitán de las Flores,[4] they called the town. The land of primitive communism, where life was the color of fiestas and simple but sophisticated people carried on a millennial struggle against mestizo oppression. Bohemian Shangri La, a place of outré fiestas, drunken orgies, and *toloache*.[5] Hundreds of dissident anthropologists, curious journalists, feminist intellectuals, gay activists, and thrill-seekers came to Juchitán in search of indigenous mystique and radical chic. Many found it. But this would be clear to me later. In July 1981 my mind was occupied with my recent marriage and my efforts to fend off recurring stomach problems caused by the bacteria-laden Isth-mus water.

As our Mexico City friends maneuvered their VW bug through the crowded Juchitán streets, I noticed political graffiti, "¡*Viva la COCEI!*" scrawled on whitewashed brick walls. A sign proclaiming *Sicarú Guyé*—"Have a Nice Trip!" in Zapotec—greeted arrivals to town. After we passed the bus station we were stopped by dissident stu-dents wearing scarlet bandannas and holding a rope across the street until we dropped a few pesos into their bucket. At the time I barely re-alized I was in COCEI territory, radical peasant country. Our breakfast of hot chocolate and tamales wrapped in banana leaves served by a beefy Juchiteca[6] marketwoman was tasty, but uneventful. The political significance of the People's Government—housed directly above us in the elegant but decayed City Hall that sheltered market stalls under its arches—was still a mystery to me. All I saw at the time was a big, dirty Indian town with a market reeking of rotting seafood, moldy cheese, basil branches, and *coyol.*[7] Aggressive marketwomen bustled everywhere in their colorful attire. My first impression of Juchitán was that it was an interesting example of urban Indian culture, nothing more.

In subsequent trips to Mexico I began to learn about Juchitán. My first glimpses of COCEI—aside from the student activists blocking the road—were front-page headlines and photographs in *Excélsior* and *Proceso* articles that I read the summer of 1983.[8] The stories and photos detailing huge COCEI political demonstrations and street fighting between *coceístas, priístas* and soldiers ignited me.[9] On my last visit to San Blas, I listened to a radio program emanating from Juchitán and filled with impassioned left-wing rhetoric. I did not realize I had tuned in to *Radio Ayuntamiento Popular,* COCEI's underground radio station. While in San Blas I heard reports of violence in Juchitán but I did not comprehend what was happening. I remember coming back to San Blas and seeing a scruffy newspaper hawker selling an extra afternoon edition of a local paper giving details about the trouble in Juchitán. I bought and read the sensational tract but could not make much sense of it. The local people told me the Juchitecos were rebels and ruffians. I assumed that was why everyone had shut themselves in their homes. At the time it seemed like some vague political unrest.

As I read the Mexico City newspapers, I began to realize that something more significant was occurring: a full-blown Indian revolt was beginning in modern Mexico! Not only that but it was occurring right under my nose in the Isthmus; its protagonists were Zapotec people, like my wife. That explained the edgy fear at the bus station in Juchitán and the military blockades and soldiers I saw as we travelled back to Mexico City by bus. As I prowled the bookstores of Mexico City in 1983 and 1984, I began to find and collect copies of *Guchachi' Reza,* a brightly illustrated Zapotec cultural magazine filled with pro-COCEI political statements, lyrical poetry, and documents concerned with Oaxaca history. I also encountered leftist and academic articles, books, and pamphlets dealing with COCEI's struggle against the PRI. Exhilarated, I realized I had a dissertation topic! But more than that, I had a mission, a goal, an obsession. I would do fieldwork on a radical Indian political movement that challenged the repressive Mexican government.

NOTES

1. Blaseños are the native people of San Blas, Oaxaca.
2. Tehuanos(as) are residents of Tehuantepec, Oaxaca.
3. A *madrina* is a godmother.
4. Juchitán of the Flowers.
5. *Toloache* is jimson weed, a narcotic plant used by Zapotec women to put men under spells and control them sexually (according to local folklore).
6. Juchitecos are the people of Juchitán. Juchiteca is the feminine form and Juchiteco is the masculine.
7. A type of palm leaf.
8. *Excélsior* is a major Mexican newspaper. *Proceso* is the most widely read political magazine in the country.
9. *Coceístas* are supporters of COCEI. *Priístas* are members of the PRI.

CHAPTER 2

Fieldwork in Juchitán and San Blas

A s I gathered my thoughts about my future fieldwork and discussed them with my professors and fellow graduate students at Wisconsin in the mid-1980s, I received a lot of helpful advice and two reactions that were not of much help. One reaction was a Madison hyper-leftist view. From that standpoint my ideas were insufficiently radical, I was not the right kind of Marxist. Although the University of Wisconsin was a great place to go to graduate school, its most troubling feature, besides the frigid midwestern winters, was the emerging "politically correct" movement.[1] Graduate seminars were informative and challenging, but sometimes degenerated into one-upmanship contests in which the goal was to show who was the most avant-garde, or at least who could strike the most elegant engagé postures. There were constant idealistic political debates about South Africa and Third World peasants, few of which had any relationship to local reality, except to the reality that mattered most to professors and graduate students: academic advancement. By the late 1980s, I would watch in amazement as many of the erstwhile Marxist-Leninists would shift to Foucaldian and Derridaean approaches without skipping a beat. One paradigm was simply replaced by another. Peasant garb was exchanged for black clothing and French cigarettes.

I do not claim to be superior to those who exchanged German for French theory. Nor was I any less zealous in my intellectual pursuits: for

me the study of a radical peasant movement was, for better or worse, a
kind of moral crusade. And the hothouse Madison intellectual scene
was the ideal point of departure for fieldwork on peasant mobilization.

The second criticism I faced was that I was too narrowly focused on
Zapotec culture. A valid criticism. However, having been enchanted by
my visits to the Isthmus, being married into a Zapotec family, and having discovered an ideal thesis topic, I was hardly about to switch my
ethnographic area to Africa or Oceania. Juchitán it would be, until I
got the COCEI out of my system.

Prior to meeting Obdulia, I had never been to Oaxaca. We met at a
language school in Mexico City. Later she took me to meet her family
and slowly I learned about the vibrant Zapotec culture of the Isthmus.
Most of what I knew initially was through contact with her family and
friends in San Blas. My knowledge of Juchitán was restricted to occasional visits and what I had read in the news media about COCEI's
conflict with the Mexican government.

My initial inquiries in Mexico in preparation for my fieldwork in
1987 were intriguing but intimidating. I spoke with my academic advi-
sor in Mexico City, Roger Bartra, the distinguished anthropologist and
social critic. Bartra said that everything would work out for me but I
should let my Zapotec interviewees know that I would be a *preguntón*,
constantly asking questions and meddling in their business. This was
sound advice, but I was not sure how much to expose my anthropological intentions in the context of violence and political repression that
prevailed in Mexico in the 1980s. The Cold War was not yet over and
Mexico had always been a battleground for political espionage by Rus-
sians, Americans, and, of course, the Mexican political police and spies
from Gobernación.[2] I was afraid that if I announced my research intentions too openly I would be harassed by Mexican undercover agents,
the U.S. Embassy, or simply mistrusted by members of the COCEI.
These were, in fact, realistic fears. My nervousness was not helped by
the warning I received from my friend Güido Munch, a veteran anthropologist at the Universidad Nacional Autónoma de México (UNAM)
who had published a book and numerous articles about the Isthmus.
Munch, in his mysterious but charming way, advised me never to share
my true feelings (about my research or anything else) with anyone, not
even my wife. He said that that was the Mexican way and that I should
play by the local rules. Good, albeit depressing, advice.

My first research forays into Juchitán were frustrating. As always I
would arrive by bus from Mexico City, an exhausting all-night ride that

thrust me into the torrid Isthmus air and humidity, hungover from lack of sleep and being scrunched into a seat built for average Mexicans, not for a 6'3" gringo. But I was always excited when I reached the Isthmus coast. Despite my fatigue, the alluring tropical smells were what hit me first: jasmine, bougainvillea, frangipani, and then of course, salty sea breezes, the aroma of wet creosote bush and the ubiquitous stench of dead dog. Arriving to the Juchitán and Tehuantepec bus stations, I was immediately immersed into the Zapotec cultural world by the jocular young women who tugged on my shirt and insisted that I buy their *quesadillas de elote* (a kind of sweet corn bread) or bright red hammocks.

On my first day of fieldwork in Juchitán, as I leaned against a car sizing up this Indian city that would obsess me for the next ten years, a Juchiteca market vendor came walking down the street toward me. I went out of my way to greet her in hopes of beginning rapport with the "native" people. Her response: she stared at me and said *"güero"* (blondie) in a loud voice, marking her territory and indicating that I was an intruder, and then briskly marched off to the market. This was hardly a promising gambit.

My first intellectual contact was with Macario Matus, a brilliant, hard-drinking poet, art critic, and director of the Juchitán Cultural Center, who would later become my key informant. Macario was friendly and receptive to my research proposal, although he later wrote me that he had initially believed that I was "one of those untrustworthy types, especially in Juchitán, who carry a red briefcase made of deerskin from the Alps, and a García Márquez-style *guayabera*." Azteca de Gyves, Macario's charming secretary, arranged for me to meet her brother, one of the three main COCEI leaders and the mayor of Juchitán during the *Ayuntamiento Popular.* What a breakthrough, connections to key figures in the Zapotec political and cultural movement! The rest would be easy. Of course it did not work out that way, but it was an auspicious beginning.

The first COCEI demonstration I attended was an eye-opener. The demonstration was held at the COCEI office on Adolfo C. Gurrión street that eventually became a popular cantina. The street was long and narrow and it was packed to overflowing with Zapotec peasants wearing their trademark huaraches; dark, cheaply tailored pants; inexpensive long-sleeved shirts; and red bandannas around their necks. The women were decked out in red *huipiles* (blouses) and *faldas* (skirts) as if to attend a fiesta. I crouched in the shade of a flowering tree and waited along with the rest of the crowd for the COCEI leaders to begin their speeches. This was one of the first rallies after the Mexican military had taken over Juchitán, so it was a semi-clandestine event.[3] The atmosphere was tense but exhilarating, the late morning sun made more bearable by the iced *horchata* (a milky, rice beverage) cleverly sold by an astute vendor as "COCEI *horchata*." The demonstration was scheduled for ten o'clock, but typical of COCEI events, did not begin until two hours later.

I waited in the crowd, nervous about being the only gringo—would the Indian radicals run me out, would Gobernación spies follow me around? These concerns contributed to my gushing perspiration from the ninety-degree heat and ninety-five-percent humidity. I tried to act nonchalant, but kept my eyes focused on the doorway of the low-slung adobe headquarters of the COCEI. Marimba music and Isthmus folksongs wafted over the loudspeakers and the crowd buzzed with conversation and laughter. Little by little, contingents of peasants arrived crowded on the flatbeds of half-ton pick-up trucks. The door that led into the labyrinthine COCEI bunker was crowded with leftist celebrities and *chilango*[4] photographers, some of them sporting tattoos, sunglassses propped on their foreheads, and jaunty postures that reminded me of world-weary Vietnam war photographers. I also spotted Pablo Gómez, a tall, imposing man with a thick black mustache— one of the leaders of the Mexican Communist Party.

Finally, the growing excitement was broken by the appearance of Leopoldo de Gyves de la Cruz (Polín), the deposed mayor of COCEI's People's Government and a national leftist folk hero. I will never forget the thrill of listening to that first COCEI speech delivered by the stunningly handsome young Indian politician. Polín's adventures with women are legendary, hardly surprising given his charisma and power. He was like a Zapotec James Dean: thin, strong, perfectly proportioned, with a distinctive high-cheeked profile. Supremely confident and relaxed, he wore his shirt sleeves rolled up on his forearms and his shirttail untucked. Polín's oratorical abilities in Spanish and Zapotec complemented his striking physical appearance. He held the audience in the palm of his hand with a careful combination of righteous denunciations of the PRI/government[5] and calls for political revenge and defense of the Isthmus homeland and Zapotec culture. His clever puns and wordplay in the indigenous language relieved the crescendoes of anger and tension that mounted as we applauded his brilliant verbal display.

The event electrified me. The heat, the sweaty communitas of the crowd, Polín's cocky charisma, and his almost erotic relationship to the COCEI masses stimulated my mind and libido. I not only wanted to become a COCEI supporter and fight the good fight against oppression, I wanted to be Polín! I wanted to be the radical golden boy wooing his supporters into battle! Eventually, I would attend dozens of COCEI rallies but I would never fail to be amazed and enthralled by the enthusiasm they generated in the COCEI rank-and-file, and in me. There is no question that part of COCEI's appeal, both locally and nationally, was the erotic dimension of the movement. Three of the main COCEI leaders positively exuded sexuality: Polín with his boyish, athletic swagger; Héctor Sánchez, the stocky, macho *jefe máximo* with his curly moustache, thick head of hair, and comely hooked nose; and Oscar Cruz, Héctor's brilliant aide-de-camp, a man's man whose vise-grip handshake and warm smile instantly won you to his side and belied his toughness, a product of street-fighting, political imprisonment, and staring down the gun barrels of PRI hitmen and soldiers. No wonder the COCEI leadership was always surrounded by groupies. European radical women, *chilanga* journalists and activists, and gringa scholars just could not get enough of the charming Zapotec politicians.

I found myself in a quandary amid the radical paparazzi, burly Zapotec bodyguards, and hip insiders. How could I gain access to the inner world of the movement and its leaders? I could hardly attempt to sneak into the COCEI inner sanctum. I was undoubtedly one of the two or three tallest people in the entire Isthmus, and white to boot. I could not sleep my way to the top as the female groupies could. My only calling card was the semi-insider status I had in San Blas due to my marriage into a Zapotec family. My other advantage was having solid grant funding that allowed me simply to stay until my repeated requests for interviews and information became less threatening and finally tolerable. These two factors were critical to my ultimate research success, along with the sincere friendships I subsequently developed with several dozen COCEI activists and Zapotec artists and intellectuals. Or maybe it was as one of my friends and informants jokingly put it one day in a cantina: "*tienes una sola virtud . . . invitas la cerveza*" (you have only one virtue . . . you buy the beer).

Cantinas, cantinas. In graduate school I was told that Latin America was a bastion of male privilege and power, that cantinas were the primary domain of machismo. The Mexican man, according to this view, specialized in excessive drinking and wife-beating. One particularly "progressive" female student once said in a seminar that the only hope for Latin American Indian women was to leave their villages and form separate all-women communes. The male participants in the seminar, likewise, competed to see who could be the most "sensitive" to women's issues. In this rarefied atmosphere we were all ideologically pure. The operative image of cantinas in the seminars was like that of Malcolm Lowry in *Under the Volcano* (1962, 204):

It was a strange place, a place really of the late night and early dawn, which as a rule, like that one other terrible *cantina*[6] in Oaxaca did not open till four o'clock in the morning. But today being the holiday for the dead it would not close. At first it had appeared to him tiny. Only after he had grown to know it well had he discovered how far back it ran, that it was really composed of numerous little rooms, each smaller and darker than the last, opening one into another, the last and darkest of all being no larger than a cell. These rooms struck him as spots where diabolical plots must be hatched, atrocious murders planned; here, as when Saturn was in Capricorn, life reached bottom.

When I started the main period of my fieldwork in May 1987, I soon learned that obtaining interviews with the COCEI leadership would be difficult. I was able to talk to some of them at demonstrations and even tagged along to federal deputy Héctor Sánchez's house after one rally. But requests for interviews were politely ignored or avoided. I was left with time on my hands and no choice but to seek other ways of gaining access to the movement. As I developed friendships with various Zapotec intellectuals at the Juchitán Cultural Center I soon learned that most afternoons, at around noon or one o'clock, a group of painters, poets, political activists, and miscellaneous bohemians and hangers-on gathered and then wandered over to a nearby cantina such as the Flor de Cheguigo, the Bar Jardín, Ra Bache'za,' or El Carrusel. I quickly became a part of this group, which we began to refer to as our "*palomilla*" or simply "*la flota*" (both expressions are roughly equivalent to "the gang" or "the guys").

Cantinas in the Isthmus, contrary to what I was told in graduate school, were often run by women (*cantineras*) and many made a tidy profit. But in other ways, the cantinas did conform to stereotype. They were, except for *cantineras*, prostitutes, and bar maids (who were also assumed to be available for a price), a male-only space. Horror of horrors! Yet the more time I spent in cantinas, the more I enjoyed them. Their sole purpose was pleasure and male bonding. Afternoons in cantinas were devoted to hedonism, leisure, joking, laughing, and alcohol-induced euphoria. I loved to grab my beer, swirl it around first like the peasants did, spit a gob of saliva on the floor, and take a big swig. Finish a bottle, bang on the metal table and the bartender would bring you another ice-cold one. Charles Bukowski would have loved those Isthmus cantinas. Unbridled down-and-dirty masculinity. The dreaded patriarchy I had been taught to loathe at school. Yet, I liked the cantinas.

The more I enjoyed the cantinas the more I realized that there was something wrong with Madison political correctness. The whole way of thinking was just too puritanical and self-righteous. There were some political philosophies that were right and true, some words a stylish progressive should use and others he or she should not, and so forth. There was a lot of talk about what was wrong with far away Third World places like Juchitán, accompanied by a kind of pseudo-sensitivity about cultural Others and calls for radical social change. This high-minded talk was of little use in "the field."[7]

What I appreciated most about the Zapotec cantinas was the camaraderie. Usually we were a group of six or seven and the crowd would grow larger or smaller as men came and went. The drinks, mainly Coronas chilled in metal ice chests, or smoky Oaxacan mescal, were paid for collectively. Each person, except for notorious deadbeats, would chip in a few pesos, or if someone was flush they would pay for everything. As the lone gringo anthropologist I often saw my friends look down at their feet or rush to the bathroom (usually a small room with a cement trough with a hole called a *mingitorio*) to avoid paying the bill. Goofy, ribald behavior was the norm. Jokes and ribbing circulated endlessly. There was, in fact, little of the macho boasting and fighting I had been led to believe were the main events at such bars.

The indigenous cantinas, especially, were also cultural centers. Itinerant musicians continually poked their heads into the bars and played a wide range of songs, many of them traditional corridos and *sones* in the indigenous language. The cantinas sustained many of the local musicians and were the breeding grounds for some of the best Isthmus songwriters, such as Rey Baxa and Saúl Martínez.

One could also eat, and eat well, in the cantinas for a pittance. Most served *botanas,* tasty items such as salted shrimp, boiled turtle eggs (sold illegally), whole fried fish, peanuts with toasted garlic and chile powder, a kind of poor man's caviar called *hueva, chicharrón* (fried pork rinds) with sliced avocado and salsa, and even stewed iguana. There were cheap, harsh Mexican cigarettes such as Delicados and Faros available. The more adventurous could easily obtain strong Oaxacan marijuana or Colombian cocaine from the local military barracks, conveniently located near some of the main bars. So there was nothing to do in the cantinas but enjoy one's self leisurely as the time went by between slugs of beer, loud guffaws, and back-slapping. Although much of the conversation focused on humor, there was also plenty of time to discuss local politics, folklore, history, and customs along with general gossip. Indeed, over time, I collected good ethnographic information in the bars. I was so obsessed with my fieldwork that four or five hours of cantina beer drinking would not stop me from immediately scribbling quotes and data in my field notebook as soon as I left the bar. Often, I wrote my notes in the quiet solitude of a church or in the near darkness of the back of a bouncy trans-Isthmus bus as I returned home to San Blas at night. I trained myself to remember the key points of discussion despite seven or eight beers over the course of those lazy Isthmus afternoons.

Note taking was frequently a precarious business. There were few times when I could sit down at a table or desk and calmly write out fieldnotes in complete sentences. Much of my data came from conversations while walking around Juchitán or loud, rowdy discussions with a gang of friends at a fiesta or family gathering. Any verbal interaction was a source of information. My note taking usually took place after the fact in the first available locale where no one would feel threatened by a gringo writing in his notebook. Much of my notes consisted of rough ideas and a kind of primitive shorthand that I would elaborate on when I got home from a day of interviews or talk in a cantina.

Lest I appear to whitewash the problems created by machismo, patriarchy, and alcoholism, I should also discuss some of the dark aspects of the cantina scene. The worst aspect of the cantinas, from a humanitarian standpoint, was the large amount of time and money that men spent on themselves instead of devoting it to their families. There were also fights and occasional acts of violence in cantinas, but these troubles were seldom started by the bohemian intellectuals I hung out with. They were more likely too busy sketching in their notebooks, reciting a poem, or painting a mural on the cantina wall in exchange for free drinks. Alcoholism was a more serious problem. Ginsberg's lines in *Howl* about seeing the best minds of his generation destroyed by alcohol and drugs were equally applicable in the Isthmus. Jesús Urbieta, a uniquely talented Zapotec painter who was on his way to becoming another Tamayo or Toledo, drank himself to death at the age of 38.

Nazario Chacón Pineda, one of the early Zapotec poets and a contemporary of Covarrubias and Rivera, was reduced to a pathetic beggar in the cantinas by the time I saw him. "El Diablo," so-called because he entered the bars and harassed and insulted you until you gave him money to buy mescal, had once been a promising student in Mexico City. Even my key informant was uselessly drunk after four o'clock every afternoon. The casualties from Isthmus drinking are too numerous to mention. Yet, done in moderation, or rather controlled excess, the communal drinking scene was a riot. It made my fieldwork not only interesting but a pleasure. And it made it possible for me to discuss politics with my informants in a tension-free atmosphere.

The whorehouse cantinas were another arena for unbridled hedonism in the Isthmus. In Salina Cruz's cavernous King Kong Club, more than one hundred numbered rooms—each equipped with a pedestal fan to ward off the torrid coastal heat—beckoned the libidinous to satisfy their desires for a mere ten dollars, more or less. At Juchitán's *La Casa Verde* (The Green House, named after Vargas Llosa's legendary brothel novel) one could get a drink and go off to the back rooms beginning about nine in the morning and continuing long into the night. One time I saw a towering Afro-Mexican woman from the Costa Chica region of Oaxaca (heavily populated by descendants of slaves who mixed with the indigenous Triques and Amuzgos) go off to one of *Casa Verde*'s cribs with a short, elderly Zapotec man. The contrast between the young, powerfully built black prostitute and the diminutive brown peasant was startling. Another prostitute was a beautiful woman from Chiapas who had been seriously injured in a car accident and braced herself on a tropical hardwood cane as she worked in the cantina. The back rooms reeked of hormones, marijuana, and the humid Isthmus air. Marimba music tinkled in the background. The atmosphere was straight out of a Fellini film.

My academic education condemned such institutions as sites of patriarchal oppresssion, but my anthropological curiosity compelled me to explore all sides of the scene from seamy to sublime. One bit of anthropological data I soon picked up in the cantinas was that many of the prostitutes in the Isthmus cantinas were from Central America, mainly Guatemala and El Salvador. What was especially interesting about this was that the women were almost exclusively mestizas (non-Indians) and their clients were primarily Zapotec Indians, in an interesting reversal of the usual Latin American race/status hierarchy. Most of the Central American women had come to the Isthmus deliberately to work in the cantinas in order to escape the extreme poverty of their countries. Others were migrants on their way to seek jobs in the United States who had run out of money.

Some cantina workers marry indigenous men they meet at the bars. This was the case of a friend of mine from Guatemala who had met her Isthmus husband in a cantina. Another male friend had a girlfriend from El Salvador who was a working bar girl. I recall a noted U.S. specialist on prostitution in Latin America pontificating about how prostitution was always an act of oppression in which the women received no sexual pleasure. Such righteous Madison-style armchair observations were precisely what I wanted to escape. The brothel cantinas, however grungy and sordid, were nonetheless part of the human experience in the Isthmus that, as an anthropologist, I could not ignore. The irony of rampant prostitution amidst a supposedly matriarchal society did not elude me. The only way to understand it was by, to quote Geertz, "being there."[8]

I especially enjoyed one incident in a roadside cantina outside of Tehuantepec. A bar girl was doing a striptease for a drunken male audience. The palm thatch and *carrizo*[9] walls barely obscured the view of travellers passing by on the Pan American Highway. As the dance continued, one drunken reveller got up from his table of friends and danced wildly with the stripper. Eventually he removed her clothing and began performing oral sex on her to her apparent delight and to that of the audience as well. What struck me about the scene was how playful rather than sexual it all was. Eventually the stripper took the man's clothing off and performed oral sex on him. Then she goaded him to fornicate with her on the floor. The whole time the guy made wild leers and bragged in an exaggerated way about his sexual prowess. But he was too drunk to perform and we all laughed as he took a bow and returned to his seat at the table with his drinking buddies. The man was neither embarrassed nor ashamed by his inability to perform. The whole thing was just clowning around rather than lurid pornography. I shudder to imagine what the right-thinking Puritans of the radical right or moralistic feminist left in the United States would have made of this display. To me, at least, it showed that sex did not always have to be so deadly serious, as in the U.S. culture wars. It could also be a source of ludic fun.[10]

In fact, I started to realize during my fieldwork that anthropology did not have to be *just* work, clinical ethnographic interviews and dry observation. Much of my best information came from rowdy political demonstrations, hallucinatory cantina binges, and the Dionysian Zapotec *velas* (fiestas). In these free-wheeling environments I was able to establish enduring friendships that provided me with deep insights into Isthmus cultural and political dynamics. People acted freely at the fiestas and other social gatherings, uninhibited by the strictures of the artificial interview setting.

The Isthmus *velas* are well known in Mexico and to foreign tourists as some of the oldest and most colorful Mexican fiestas. The *vela* organizers (*mayordomos*) begin preparation for the events a year in advance. When the big day comes (actually many *velas* carry on for two or three days) all other activities are set aside as women deck themselves in their finest *trajes,* gold necklaces, and bangle earrings. They often adorn their hair with flowers and ribbons and go to great lengths to outdo their rivals to shine in the eyes of the fiesta guests. Several streets are blocked off for the events, and an *enramada* made of crooked wooden poles and palm leaves is constructed to protect the participants from the harsh Tehuantepec winds. At one end of the *enramada*, a bandstand is set up for the various groups and orchestras to play tropical music and Zapotec *sones* for dancing and the enjoyment of the hundreds of guests who sit around the *enramada* in wooden or metal folding chairs swigging iced beers and eating delicacies like iguana tamales, spicy stews, and seafood fried in garlic.

The *velas* are carefully choreographed, from the triumphant entrances of the women, gaudy as peacocks, to the twirling petticoats and skip-and-hop dancing, to traditional *sones,* and finally to the ceremonial passing on of *vela* sponsorship from current to future *mayordomos.* The *velas* usually start around ten in the evening and carry on all night or into the next day at the *lavada de olla* (the ritualized cleaning of the dirty stew pots). As the night wears on and heavy drinking starts to take effect, the *velas* take on an atmosphere of Brazilian carnivals or a scene out of Hieronymous Bosch. People drink and dance with their friends until they are exhausted; the excessively tired pass out on the ground. Sloppy fistfights occasionally mar the fun. Much of the dancing is done by women, who are the most visible and the true stars of the *velas.* Men sit around drinking, joking, and gossiping.

In August 1987, soon after I started my research, Obdulia and I attended an important *vela* in Santa María, the largest of Tehuantepec's approximately fourteen barrios. Santa María's fiesta events center around two groups, "The Societies of the South and the North,"[11] which roughly correspond with geographical divisions of the barrio.

The two groups feign an ancestral hostility and try to outdo each other in festive preparations and in the elaborateness of their respective parties. Although the tension between the two societies is an artificial, "invented tradition," the fiesta itself has considerable longevity. Occasionally the sponsors of previous fiestas are named publicly; in one case, a list of sponsors dating back to 1912 was read aloud to the people attending the event.

We arrived at Santa María in the early evening at which time there was riotous dancing going on under a "*stand*," a metal structure which is slowly replacing the *enramadas* of traditional fiestas. The two societies each had their own *stand*, band, and membership. The two *stands*, however, rested side by side and both parties tended to overlap slightly, although an effort was maintained to show disinterest or disdain for the other group's party. Approximately 2,000 people were in attendance, many of whom were drinking beer and brandy. Women were dressed in *trajes* and men wore their best clothes; some men had red bandannas around their necks.

Suddenly, the two groups yelled insults and jeers at each other, and *vivas* for their own group. Then, each of the two societies passed out sugar cane staves, *ocote* stick torches, and a type of papier-mâché bulb called a *marmota* which had a candle on the inside for a light source. The two groups then took off on marches in different directions and waved the sugar cane and torches while insulting, cursing, and defaming the opposition, albeit in jest. Along the route they shouted *vivas*, *mueras*, and *arribas*.[12]

After some time, the Society of the South arrived at the house of one of their group leaders who had created a display of colored light bulbs with the society's name on the house's second floor balcony. Some celebrants exploded firecrackers, others drank toasts, and the rest began dancing to recorded music. Several participants shouted more *vivas* and *mueras*. Next, a structure (known as a *torito*) of cane stalks, papier-mâché and firecrackers was brought out and a man danced around with it on his head.

The Society of the North marched through the northern end of town and then returned to the bandstand area (in front of the Santa María church). Music began again—each society had its own electric and acoustic bands—and dancing resumed, culminating in the lighting of the *torito* by the northern group. The firecracker bull shot off smoke and firecrackers as the man who was supporting it danced wildly around the bandstand area sending colored sparks all over the place.

When the north's *torito* burned out they lighted their *castillo,* a ten-meter high scaffolding of cane or bamboo which supported a diverse array of fireworks including spinning devices, firecrackers, flares, Whistling Petes, and bottle rockets.

The huge crowd was crammed together close to the *castillo.* Although professionally constructed, the *castillo* posed a considerable health hazard since it was located near electric power lines, houses, and the fiesta goers. A serious malfunction could have injured hundreds of people. In fact, sparks, ash, and debris from the north's *castillo* landed on the crowd but it did not cause significant injury. Obviously, Oaxacan fiestas are not tightly controlled by government safety laws. Events such as this fiesta produce a kind of reckless abandon that is exhilarating and potentially dangerous. A brawl or other disturbance at a fiesta could injure many people or set off a calamitous stampede.

After the northern society finished burning their fireworks, the southern group lit their impressive *castillo,* which clearly outclassed that of the north with a creative combination of burning crowns, doves, and hearts, and exciting displays of firecracker pyrotechnics ending with a burning hoop which shot into the sky and exploded in a burst of color. After this display, the party continued into the early morning hours. The success of the south's *castillo* brought the applause and whoops of its supporters who gloated in their success and trumping of their mock rivals. We left the fiesta at about midnight, thoroughly exhausted.[13]

Isthmus fiestas, though tiring, were an ideal venue for establishing rapport and learning cultural information. My only problem was how to retain it all as I drank beer after cold beer. In early September 1987 I attended three *velas* in a row in Juchitán: the *Vela Pineda, Vela 5 de Septiembre,* and *Vela López.* After three nights of intense partying and only a few hours of boozy sleep in the Isthmus heat, I was wiped out and had to spend the next three days recuperating. This respite gave me free time to write field notes and collect memories of the bits and pieces of data I had gleaned at the *velas.* That was how my fieldwork went: periods of frenetic activity, punctuated by lulls in which I refined my notes at home and worried about whether I was a good anthropologist.

The slow pace of life in San Blas was a perfect antidote to tense or hectic days of research in Juchitán. In Juchitán, away from my in-laws, I was not as well-known and my gringo identity was more conspicuous, hence I felt less secure. Because Juchitán was fifteen miles away from San Blas, and I was expected to return home each night, I had to take advantage of each free hour among the Juchitecos to establish new contacts, conduct interviews, collect notes from newspapers, and attend demonstrations. In San Blas, I typed data into a computer at a leisurely clip and, when in need of a rest, stuck my head out the *zaguán* and observed all kinds of interesting Zapotec cultural activities.

At the time of my dissertation research, most of San Blas was unpaved except for Hidalgo and Francisco Cortés streets. Even the paved streets were partially covered with sand, mud, and garbage, which was always shifting due to the incessant winds and sporadic rain. Blowing sand and grit in the streets during the windy season was an unrelenting nuisance to eyes, clothes, and houses. San Blas had a patched, raggedy appearance due to the ever-present house construction projects and haphazardly strung electric and telephone lines. The streets were mostly narrow—about fifteen feet wide—which was adequate for foot traffic, bicycles, and oxcarts, but with the advent of cars and *motos* (motorized three-wheel vehicles with a flat bed for cargo on the back), had become insufficient. The *motos,* which used tiny, grossly overloaded motorcycle engines, were a persistent source of noise and pollution; however, they were very manueverable in San Blas's dirty, crowded, and winding streets.

The streets were the primary playground for young kids, who created a lively show for onlookers. Blaseño children invented unusual games such as *caratela,* which is simply a piece of wire with a hook on it which guides a round metal hoop as in curling. Another toy was a cane pole with a string or rag attached to it that was pulled between the legs like a horse. Six o'clock in the afternoon was the primary time for children to play in the streets, because the hot sun began to go down and the day finally cooled. It was also a key time for socializing since many of the day's activities ceased at that point. Many houses had low concrete porches whose principal function was as a place for sitting and conversing in the evening (as well as off and on throughout the day).

At least once a week, funeral processions passed our house on the way to the church. Zapotec men, wearing *guayabera* shirts and dark pants, led the processions. The closest male relatives carried the casket and the women, dressed in black or purple *huipiles* and rebozos, followed the men. The ubiquitous brass band, composed of one tuba and various trumpets, saxophones, and other horned instruments, sweating profusely in the Isthmus sun, brought up the rear blaring traditional tunes. The schmaltzy oompahs of the band were periodically interrupted by the shrieks and mournful cries of the widow, mother, or

other kinswomen of the deceased. The bereaved woman, physically im-
molated by suffering, draped her arms over the shoulder of her relatives, and would have to be dragged or carried along. A more dramatic
illustration of the tragedy of death would be hard to imagine. From every house, bystanders, such as myself, stuck their heads out windows
and front doors and watched the passing processions, almost as a kind
of grim spectator sport. On everyone's lips were the names of the dead
and the causes of death.

On the Day of the Dead such lugubrious proceedings were only
slightly lessened by candles, food, and flower adornments, and the
drunken cries of musicians and loved ones as they serenaded the deceased while standing on their grave. Early in my fieldwork, I attended
a Day of the Dead celebration at the San Blas cemetery that was a profound statement about Zapotec people's reverence for their relatives, a
feeling that is best described as ancestor worship. The cemetery was
filled with plants and trees in a natural setting surrounded by Jaguar
Hill and peasant corn fields, in stark contrast to the neatly trimmed
lawns and artificial environment of U.S. cemeteries. San Blas's cemetery is located on the outskirts of town in a liminal zone that divides the
community from the fields. The area has a mysterious quality that is
heightened by local folklore about eerie and illegal goings-on in the vi-
cinity. Some of the tombs have elaborate painted concrete and plaster
gravestones or monuments, but most simply consist of a wooden or
metal cross and a dirt area marked by a stone or brick outline of where
the dead person was buried. In the little chapel at the cemetery there
was an altar covered with marigold flowers and crosses. A pile of dirt lay
on the ground in front of the altar in the form of a grave.

When Obdulia and I arrived, there were hundreds of people, mainly
women, crowding in through the stone entrance. Typical of Isthmus
social events, women sold beverages and food (mostly pastries). This
particular day, two funerals were held. One was of the former owner of
"The Dominantes" musical group. Except for the men at the burials,
the rest of the people at the cemetery were women. A sensuous mixture
of winter winds, deep blue sky, billowy white clouds, and the sharp
green hues of nearby corn patches and coconut palms enlivened the
setting. The visual display was accentuated by women's colorful
huipiles, orange marigold flowers, shocking reddish-purple *cresta de
gallo* (cockscomb) flowers, and green and red *coquito* (palm) leaves.
Marimba music drifted over a loudspeaker, while a brass band played
music atop the grave of the deceased leader of "The Dominantes." The

lead singer crooned songs of sorrow in honor of his dead friend. In the background, wails and sobs of female relatives formed an impromptu chorus. The people, noise, and activity made the occasion simultaneously festive and solemn. Grief and sadness marked the faces of many, while others lightened the mood with humor and soft conversation.

Zapotec women arrived at the cemetery with buckets or baskets of flowers which they took to their relatives' graves along with a machete which they used to clean up the tomb and cut back wild plants. The women placed their flowers on a grave or tied them to a wooden or metal cross. Water to freshen the flowers was obtained from a tank located near the entrance. Some women cried and whispered to their buried relatives. Others said prayers or asked for forgiveness for having neglected or mistreated the deceased, or for having betrayed their desires.

A group of drunken men sang, embracing each other and swaying with the music, around the tomb of the dead musician. This provided a soulful, spiritual feeling, although this effect was counteracted by another group of men who drank mescal, told jokes, and laughed. After these men left, one drunken mourner fell and struck his head on a tombstone. He lay there with dried, crusted blood on his head and clothing until another man and I dragged him out of the cemetery where he came to his senses and wandered home.

Some of the women at the cemetery took advantage of the opportunity to chat with friends, relatives, and acquaintances, or exchange news and remembrances of the dead. Having completed their grave cleaning, they left flower offerings, whispered their communications or prayers to the dead, and then walked home. We soon followed.

Constant fiesta parades through San Blas were much happier events. Typically, their arrival was announced by exploding bottle rockets followed by men on horseback; oxcarts decorated with flowers, palm leaves, and coconuts; or young women carrying brightly colored banners with garish pictures of a patron saint. The marchers were always separated by gender and age: first men then women, with each gender divided into four age groups from the oldest to the youngest.[14] In one of the most exotic marches, young girls in brilliantly shaded costumes of satin or velvet blouses embroidered with flowers, long petticoats (*the traje tehuana*), and a starched white headdress (*huipil grande*) as a halo gracefully paraded through the streets. As the march neared, children squealed with glee and scrambled to their doorsteps, adults dropped what they were doing and ran to observe the action, and even dogs rushed to be part of the scene. Friends or relatives shouted out encouragement to the marchers, neighbors cracked raucous jokes to the delight of the crowd, and members of the procession periodically shouted *vivas* to a saint or fiesta association responsible for the exciting events.

In my favorite fiesta procession, in honor of the local fishing industry, men dressed in the typical garb of fishermen (huaraches, pants rolled up to the knee, white t-shirts, and red bandannas) lugged heavy weighted fishnets that they periodically threw over the heads of the spectators, while the crowd scurried to escape the trapping nets. When they arrived at the church, the fishermen, simulating the methods of the nearby Huave, enacted the Turtle dance, in which they crouched and swept the sand for turtle eggs, a main source of livelihood for coastal Indians. Another dancer carrying a swordfish costume threatened onlookers with his long, sharp, blade-like jaw until he was caught in a fishermen's net.

On New Year's Eve, raucous street celebrations took place, including the lighting of thousands of firecrackers and bottle rockets, stuffing and burning a *viejo* (dummy of an old man) who represented the past year, and wild gunshots at midnight. An especially amusing sight was cross-dressing young boys and girls who danced suggestively and sang obscene ditties until they were given small tips. I enjoyed the heavy drinking and drunken hugging of relatives and neighbors accompanied by the compulsory exchange of "¡*Felíz Año!*" (Happy New Year!), but I ran for cover when my father-in-law and brother-in-law brought out the pistol and began firing into the air.

I seldom felt bored or lonely in San Blas, but when I did I would telephone home, which cost an astronomical fee, or I wrote lengthy letters. The occasional delivery of a letter from family and friends was a source of great satisfaction. Another regular connection with the "outside world" was the monthly arrival of my fellowship check. The first month of my research (May 1987) the check came three weeks late, which wreaked havoc on our household budget. This problem was finally straightened out after I made several angry phone calls to the Mexico City office of my sponsor, the Organization of American States.

I always felt embarrassed at the Tehuantepec bank when I collected the fellowship money. Although the amount of my monthly stipend ($450 U.S.) was not much by American standards, in Mexican currency it was the staggering sum of 900,000 pesos, which created a huge pile on the cashier's counter. After the bank clerk handed me the bills, I would sheepishly count them under the gaze of long lines of peasant farmers and townspeople, stuff the bundle loosely in my pocket, then quickly grab a taxi home.

In my free time I explored the towns of Tehuantepec and San Blas by foot. I especially enjoyed hiking from our home in San Blas over the saddle between Cruz Padre López Hill and Jaguar Hill down into the town of Tehuantepec. Although Tehuanos viewed their mestizo town as culturally superior to Indian San Blas, in reality, Tehuantepec was a sleepy, slow-moving community. The downtown area, dominated by the central park, City Hall building, and marketplace, had a lethargic, worn-out feel. Lines of taxis and *motos* baking in the tropical sun calmly awaited passengers, then buzzed off amid clouds of acrid exhaust fumes. A few shoppers strolled along the cracked, dirty sidewalks. The dusty stores around the park sold an unimaginative array of goods, the surrounding restaurants were mostly mediocre. The most interesting feature of Tehuantepec was the old two-story brick market. As it has been for centuries, the market was run primarily by women, many of them Zapotec.

Surrounding the market were a juice bar and newspaper stand where I whiled away numerous hours along with languid locals. The interior of the market, though poorly lit, was a riot of colors and odors. Along one wall on the ground floor were raw meat vendors whose bloody products were not refrigerated and gave off frightful aromas. Next to the butcher shops were stalls selling cheese and other milk products which were often stale and exuded their own strong smells. The stalls in the middle of the floor were redolent with the smells of homegrown flowers and herbs such as marigolds, gardenias, basil, oregano, carnations, roses, and hibiscus. Adjacent to the flowers and herbs, vendors displayed huge mounds of avocados, onions, tomatoes, chiles, and other fresh vegetables. The slippery floor was littered with rotting produce, meat juice, spoiled milk, and other less identifiable objects. The building buzzed with the sounds of market haggling in Spanish and Zapotec. Boisterous marketwomen transformed these conversations into lively entertainment with clever puns and loud laughter.

Up the stairwell past handicapped beggars, the second story housed mostly clothing and jewelry. The dominant aroma was the freshly cured leather of cheap huaraches. One made one's way precariously through rows of hanging dresses and other clothing, including expensive *huipiles* and *trajes*. I often navigated my way to the second floor to chat with my sister-in-law, Irene, who expertly managed a stall that sold children's clothing.

Outside the market, local women in improvised stalls sold tropical fruits such as papayas, mangos, coconuts, oranges, limes, pineapples, and *chicozapotes*. I especially enjoyed the theatrical element of bargaining. Following my mother-in-law's example, I feigned little interest in the goods, made deprecating comments about the fruit, and complained bitterly about the first offered price. After bantering awhile and seeking a lower price, I would pretend to leave in a huff, then abruptly turn around and, grudgingly, accept the final offer. I used to think I was an accomplished market consumer, until one of my Juchiteco friends pointed out that Zapotec women market vendors always got their minimum price, despite their own exaggerated complaints about being robbed by stingy buyers.

Another pleasurable diversion was a hike up Jaguar Hill to the chapel overlooking San Blas. From this vantage point, one could appreciate the natural beauty of the Isthmus: fields of tall, green coconut palms lined up like toy soldiers all the way to the sea, the snaky meandering of the Tehuantepec River, the blue and brown hues of the hulking Sierra Atravesada mountains, and the orange tile roofs of the densely packed Blaseño dwellings. Though San Blas was viewed by Tehuanos and Juchitecos as a mere village, from above, its concentrated settlement pattern gave the appearance of a small city. On one hike up the hill I was accompanied by Pedro, a neighbor boy, who, having never made the trip before was stunned by the grandeur of his hometown when seen from this standpoint. When I asked him how many houses there were, he replied, "a million."

A popular excursion from San Blas was to go swimming in the muddy waters of the nearby irrigation canal. This trip was also instructive because alongside the canal—part of the massive federally sponsored Isthmus dam and irrigation project—lay miles and miles of huge, costly concrete irrigation pipes that were never installed due to government inefficiency or corruption. Other swimming holes included the jungle oasis-like springs at Laollaga and Tlacotepec or the deep pools (known as "Las Pilas") near Mixtequilla. Las Pilas was especially enjoyable during mango season when the ripe, juicy fruit literally fell off the trees as in a Rousseau-esque paradise. Sometimes falling mangos hit unlucky bathers on the head to the delight of all present.

A day in the country on a relative's farm was another relaxing break from town life and fieldwork. Local peasant farmers till small plots of

corn typically surrounded by a rectangular or oval boundary of coconuts, mangos, and banana trees. They build small thatch huts strung
with hammocks for overnight stays. On a lazy Isthmus afternoon on
the farm, there was little to do but chase iguanas, pick bananas and
limes, eat lunch, and snore in a hammock. Oxcarts occasionally rum-
bled by, while vultures soared overhead and bees buzzed in the trees.

A more adventurous outing in the countryside took one on deeply
rutted dirt roads through the fields to lagoons and salt flats around the
Alvaro Obregón Colony or the Huave villages. The ramshackle bus
loaded with farmers and their belongings, including chickens tied by
their feet, bounced violently on the weather-beaten roads the entire
way. On one trip to the Huave town of San Mateo, I saw a local farmer
string a rope around a goat's neck and drag it, protesting, onto the roof
of the bus. En route, one encountered a few peasants working their
fields with oxteams and observed palm and woodpost dwellings,
known as *palapas,* that seemed African in style. The sandy dunes of the
Huave Indian region had a ghostly, moonlike quality. Somehow the local people keep cattle, chickens, and some pigs on this sandy soil, but
mostly they survive through fishing the lagoons and ocean waters.

The Huave people are known in Mexico as one of the most reserved,
traditional groups. Their language is unrelated to that of the surrounding indigenous cultures. Visitors to Huave towns are hardly acknowl-
edged and the quiet, inward atmosphere of the people contrasts
sharply with the loud, boisterous behavior common in Zapotec towns.
In a Huave village, simple adobe and wattle-and-daub homes are surrounded by formidable fences of spiny mesquite and other branches.
The impression is that of a people who want to be left alone, which is
understandable given their history of victimization by the Zapotecs
and Spanish. The remote, unearthly ambience is heightened by the lack
of vegetation and the unceasing gales from the Pacific Ocean.

My main contact with the Huaves came through a Zapotec fisher-
man from Alvaro Obregón, Alfredo Antonio Gómez, whose wife is a
Huave. Alfredo sold Obdulia and me some perch and red snapper from
his daily excursions to the lagoons, and we eventually became good
friends and, ultimately, *compadres.* His home is a three-bedroom brick
structure surrounded by a big open patio fenced in by ditch reeds. The
patio contains a pig pen, vegetable garden, open-air kitchen, and clay
hearth. Hammocks for sleeping and resting are strung up in the
open-air porch which is roofed but has no walls. The patio also has nu-

merous fruit trees, and chickens and turkeys roam freely around the yard.

During visits to his humble home, Alfredo taught me about the simple but colorful lives of Isthmus fishermen. He told me that most fishermen work when it is dark. Alfredo goes fishing twice a day: at five in the morning and five in the afternoon. His wife and daughters sell the fresh fish daily in San Blas. The fishermen's basic method is to stake their weighted nets into the muddy bottom of the lagoons and spend the rest of the time waiting in their boats for strikes. Often the fishermen smoke marijuana to help them withstand the tedium of the job. It is easy to imagine how ethereal the nights are for the stoned fishermen as they sit in their wooden boats with nothing around them but starry sky, winds, and lapping waves. No wonder fishermen often tell the most elaborate folktales and stories.

One afternoon, Alfredo decided to take me fishing in the lagoons near Alvaro Obregón. We drove my car along a rough dirt and sand road, then through an area of fine sand lined with spiny brush out to the salty flats next to the water. Once we got to the water's edge, Alfredo poled me out into the lagoon in his *cayuco* (dugout canoe). Alfredo purchased the twenty-five-foot-long vessel in Chiapas. It is about six feet wide and only one or two inches thick. He and his twelve-year-old son (who is now fairly accomplished at many of the fishing tasks) manuevered the canoe with long bamboo poles and a sail made from ten or more cloth pieces salvaged from sugar sacks sewn together and connected to a rough wooden mast by ropes.

Alfredo's net was made of nylon thread, ropes, and wooden weights attached to a twenty-foot-long pole. The pole, with a rag tied to it, stuck out of the water and marked the net's location. The net itself was about 200 meters long. A plastic pan was used for bailing water out of the *cayuco,* and an anchor completed the inventory of equipment. It was a very rudimentary, but efficient, system.

Other fishermen I saw had outboard motors attached to their boats. The craft were left unattended on the muddy beach of the lagoon, which seemed to indicate a degree of trust among the fishermen. About ten *cayucos* were stored in the shallow water near where we left to go fishing. Alfredo said that the fishermen respected each other's nets. There is no law or cooperative which controls this particular fishing area and that is how Alfredo liked things.

The fishing trip itself was scary due to the unrelenting high winds. At one point Alfredo's son lost one of the poles. At times I wondered whether the sail would hold up under the gusty winds. We eventually made it out to the net, with considerable effort on their part, which gave me great respect for fishermen. Perhaps as a response to the dangers of the job and the lack of fixed hours or bosses, Alfredo is very happy-go-lucky. He sang songs as we poled out into the lagoon. He said that what he does is not really work and he enjoys it although it is very dangerous. Alfredo noted how a *cayuco* had recently tipped over, killing all four of its crew. Two died when the *cayuco* landed on them, the others drowned.

During the entire voyage, the winds seemed on the verge of capsizing us. At times, the canoe could barely move forward against the vicious gusts, despite how hard we pushed and pulled with the wooden poles. When the going got rough, Alfredo called out to me and his young son to work as hard as we could "*con toda alma y vida*" (with all our soul and life). I panicked at the thought of being thrown into the turbulent water, but Alfredo never broke a sweat and not once ceased his friendly banter. Finally, we made it to the net and Alfredo dragged in a hefty catch of fresh fish. At that point, however, I was feeling seasick and only too happy to return to shore.

Before we left Alfredo, he invited us to his twin daughters' *quinceañera* (debutante party for fifteen-year-old girls). He said he was planning to have "The Fenders," a musical group from San Mateo, play at the party. They would charge 450,000 pesos which would be a huge expense for him. Alfredo said to us, in a very sincere fashion, that he wanted to be friends for life. He showed us extraordinary hospitality and gave us a big batch of fish, shrimp, and abalone. He said, "I am a poor man, but I have a big heart." Although Alfredo seemed spontaneously generous, he also let us know—in a very Isthmus-style way—that he expected reciprocity. By inviting us to his daughter's party, we would be obligated to bring a gift. As a "rich" gringo, I would be expected to buy an especially nice one. As we said goodbye, Alfredo also asked me to bring him some books so that he could "open up his mind."

After repeatedly coming to visit me in San Blas with gifts of fresh fish, Alfredo finally asked me to be his *compadre* at the *quinceañera*. I agreed, and supplied sufficiently expensive twin gold necklaces for the girls at their lavish party. The girls' costly *quinceaños* bash was especially impressive given how hard their father had to work to pay for the band, cake, liquor, and food for 100 guests. It was hard not to like an earthy man like Alfredo who confronted a difficult life with vigor and bonhomie. He used to joke that he had so many children because of his enormous penis. Like other Istmeños[15] I knew, Alfredo had no qualms when it came to joking about sexuality and body parts. When he got a break from fishing, he loved to guzzle quarts of beer, laugh hysterically, crack jokes, and tell stories.

Many Isthmus Zapotec people are consummate storytellers, as is common in rural, peasant communities with extensive oral traditions. One of the many advantages of living with my wife's family was that her parents often told me about Isthmus folklore and history at meals or during idle conversation. One night as we chatted in front of the house, my father-in-law (Roberto) and mother-in-law (Elvira) told me some interesting tales about the origins of wealth in the community. According to their version—which reflects regional, class, and ethnic tensions in Oaxaca—San Blas was, until recently, a poor, isolated town.

When Elvira and Roberto were married in 1943, there were only four light bulbs in all of San Blas and no houses had piped water. It was not until the Pan-American highway was completed, around 1960, that the area began to grow economically. Prior to the advent of the highway, there was limited delivery of goods from outside sources. Residents of the Oaxaca Valley, known derogatorily as "*Vallistos*,"[16] brought some provisions on mules and donkeys which they also rode through the rugged Oaxacan mountains to the Isthmus. Occasionally the *Vallistos* would come by horse, but these were usually too weak to manage the trip. The muleteers kept their animals in a huge stable and fed them with corn chaff and grass sold by Blaseños, who thought the *Vallistos* were a particularly squalid and pathetic lot.

Each muleteer, despite his appearance, brought a whole string of mules laden with fruit, vegetables, and other products from the valley and highlands of Oaxaca that were scarce in the Isthmus. According to my in-laws, the crafty *Vallistos* sold these wares at considerable profit and eventually acquired great wealth. They said that other extremely poor *Vallistos* have come to the Isthmus selling needles or handmade jewelry. The *Vallistos* looked forlorn as they squatted on the ground or sidewalk near Tehuantepec City Hall, eating nothing but beans and tortillas. Yet through street-vending, the *Vallistos* have supposedly become prosperous, bought nice homes, and now lead comfortable lives.

Roberto and Elvira also told the story of a *Vallisto* who worked in a sugar cane mill. He was a very poor man, but suddenly became rich. According to the *Vallisto*, every morning on his way to work he was accosted by a rooster on the pass that connects the northwest side of San

Blas with Tehuantepec. Tiring of being chased and clawed by the rooster, the *Vallisto* decided to take the rooster home with him, in other words to steal the bird. When he went to do so the rooster did not make a sound or put up a fight, so the *Vallisto* was able to carry the bird on his chest all the way home. Arriving at his house, the man realized that the whole rooster had turned to gold. And that is how the *Vallisto* became rich. Roberto was sure that the *Vallisto* had either stolen money or found it because he had previously been impoverished, but suddenly became rich.

Similar folklore surrounded the rise of Señor Gallegos, the richest man in San Blas. According to one local account, two young kids (who are old men now) were riding in a taxi with a gringo. The gringo left a briefcase or a wallet or something in the car when he left. The gringo's belongings had a large amount of money in them. The kids did not know what to do with it, so they asked Mr. Gallegos what to do. Mr. Gallegos gave them a small amount of money and kept the rest. And that is how Mr. Gallegos became rich, because formerly he was a poor silversmith.

My reading of these stories is that they are classic examples of Mesoamerican peasant folklore regarding the social mobility of a few in a mostly homogenous society. In a situation of "limited good" (Foster 1964), an individual's enrichment can only be explained by a crime or miraculous act. Such stories not only explain the source of a person's wealth, but may also harbor resentment of the prosperous, as in the case of Señor Gallegos who was accused of tricking the innocent kids into giving him the money they had found. These stories also exemplify underlying ethnic and regional conflicts: the tension between Isthmus Zapotec peasants and Valley Zapotec or non-Zapotec merchants from Central Oaxaca.

Despite its natural beauty, the Isthmus was a cauldron of political conflicts and interpersonal rivalries. Ensconced in the Ruiz family home, however, I felt quite safe. It was an excellent standpoint from which to learn about local politics and community life. My domestic arrangement was as if made-to-order for anthropological fieldwork.

NOTES

1. For a recent study of "political correctness" in the U.S. academy see Cummings (2000). Madison, Wisconsin, and the University of Wisconsin are reputed to be among the main places where "political correctness" began.

2. Often translated as the Ministry of the Interior, the Mexican *Secretaría de Gobernación* is in charge of, among other things, internal political control. At the time of my fieldwork, and probably still today, this bureaucracy had a network of political operatives and informers all over the country.

3. COCEI members won elections and took control of the Juchitán mayor's office in 1981. From 1981 to 1983, COCEI, which called its regime the "People's Government" (*Ayuntamiento Popular*), engaged in radical political projects in support of Zapotec peasants and workers. In 1983, the Mexican government, using political instability as an excuse, kicked COCEI out of office and installed soldiers in Juchitán's City Hall building. For more information on COCEI's political history see Campbell (1994) and Campbell et al. (1993).

4. *Chilangos(-as)* are residents of Mexico City. Depending on the context, this word may be used affectionately or as an insult.

5. "*PRI-Gobierno*" is a common expression used by members of Mexico's political opposition to criticize and make fun of the PRI's dominance of the Mexican governmental system. The expression implies that the PRI and the government are one and the same, which at times they appear to be.

6. Lowry italicized the word *cantina*.

7. Matt Gutmann's, in many ways insightful, book about Mexican machismo contains interesting perspectives on cantinas. This discussion, however, is weakened by his revelation that he was invited to go to cantinas only three times during his fieldwork (1996, 176). He also describes cantinas as expensive places to drink. In my experiences throughout Mexico, working-class cantinas have always been the cheapest place to drink, outside of simply buying beer from a retail store or *deposito* (beer distribution store).

8. I should point out that most cantinas are simply bars, drinking establishments without prostitutes or overt sexual interaction. Furthermore, many men spend only a few hours or even less time in the cantina on any given visit. Hence one should not assume that all or most cantina drinkers are out-of-control drunks or philanderers.

9. A kind of reed.

10. It is important, of course, to recognize that women dancing nude in bars for male pleasure occurs in a context of patriarchy and female exploitation. The woman involved in this particular incident may not have enjoyed what happened and may just have been going through the motions. But it seemed to me that she found it amusing, perhaps a moment of mirth amid a somewhat dreary existence. What I am arguing is that we try to understand the dynamics of people's lives—in cantinas or anywhere else—instead of jumping to prearranged moralistic conclusions (i.e., "political correctness").

11. "*La Sociedad del Sur y la Sociedad del Norte.*"

12. "*Muera*" means "death to (someone)," and *arriba* means "up with (someone)," in this context.

13. I abbreviated and compressed aspects of the fiesta for the sake of clarity.

14. For example, the women's section of the procession consisted of first the elderly women, then married adult women, young women, and children at the end.

15. Natives of the Isthmus.

16. The term *Vallistos* is used by Istmeños as a quasi-ethnic label to distinguish themselves from their political rivals in the Oaxaca Valley. Though *Vallistos* are often also Zapotecs (though speakers of a dialect of Zapotec that is difficult for many Isthmus natives to understand), they are usually viewed by Isthmus Zapotecs as being of a different, inferior Indian group.

CHAPTER 3

Zapotec Community and Family Life

Living with a Zapotec family was a communal experience. In practice, that meant I paid all the bills. That is the way things work, he who has the most pays the most. In other respects, we shared more equally the good and bad experiences of life, and our emotional ups and downs. Living this way was a daily exercise in cultural differences and a supply of boundless grist for the anthropological mill. Communal living was mandatory because of the very nature of our dwelling, a sprawling two-story brick house connected to my brother-in-law Octavio's small house by an open passage. The kitchen and main living spaces—the hall and patio where people lounged in *butaques*[1] (a low-slung wooden chair) or hammocks—were shared by all. In addition to the immediate family, a constant flow of relatives, friends, and neighbors came and went through the always-open *zaguán*. Food vendors would announce their presence and walk up the entrance hall with their wares: mangos, fresh pastries, shrimp, tortillas, and so on. A man whose job was to invite people to fiestas would enter and repeat a memorized invitation in a sing-song spiel, a human version of a recorded message. Small children, and even neighborhood dogs, came and went.

Obdulia and I had a small degree of privacy in our upstairs apartment, but all household residents felt free to come up at any time. Being alone is neither possible nor desirable for Zapotec people. Both village and family life in San Blas were collective experiences. One simply lived life among and around other people. This was even the case when watching television. Since our house had one of the few decent television sets on the block, the little anteroom where the television sat would fill up as the evening's *telenovelas* (soap operas) began. At the sound of the distinctive jingle of Rosa Salvaje, a popular soap opera featuring the emerging star Verónica Castro, a group of Blaseños of all ages crowded into the house, most sitting on the floor, and huddled around the television. At times there were as many as fifteen people viewing the program. The house would be much more crowded at the weekly family gatherings or birthday parties, when we would eat barbecued goat with green chile sauce and cold beer.

I eventually got used to the communal living arrangements, although it took longer to adapt to other household customs. One was that every family member had a right to ask me for money, not a loan but a gift, at any moment. It was assumed that I was wealthy since I was a gringo, and it was expected that I would share what I had. Change left over from money given to an in-law to purchase food from the market was never returned. Stealing, or rather borrowing, small household items from relatives went on constantly. The ethics of "stealing" were made clear to me by Elvira, my mother-in-law, when she told a story of how as a child, she had been sent by her mother to fetch firewood from the wild hillside. While searching for wood, Elvira came across a woodcutter who set down his bundle of sticks to go off to the bushes to relieve himself. Elvira then took the wood home to her mother. When I complained to my mother-in-law that this was wrong, she replied that she needed the wood more than the man did, hence the act was justified. She said that I was naïve and had never known poverty, thus I could not understand her motivations.

On trips to the market or stores, my relatives would often pocket a few chiles or a container of deodorant, whatever they needed at the time. In other small ways I realized that a kind of instinctive deviousness was a part of everyday life. Lies were commonplace and no one ever confessed to breaking a plate or committing some other minor foible.[2] The little store, in a front room of the family home, that Obdulia and I financed to provide a livelihood for her youngest sister, Margarita, never made a profit, since bags of rice, jars of sugar, and other food items were always being siphoned off by needy family members. Private property was simply not sacred. As I got used to these sorts of practices, adopting the anthropologist Munch's advice, I began to live like the local people, abandoning my naïve gringo innocence (another version of the holier-than-thou self-righteousness that permeates Anglo-American culture). I would even cadge a few pesos from time to time from a wealthy brother-in-law.

The daily round of life began early. Peasant wooden oxcarts noisily creaked to work at four or five in the morning to beat the fiery Isthmus afternoon heat. By five or six o'clock, adult women and girls were lined up in front of the corn mill to buy their daily rations of corn dough for tortillas. By seven or eight o'clock, the loudspeakers (rigged up to tall poles) droned out the price of bargains at the San Blas market in the sing-song rhythm of the Zapotec language. The streets were now filled with women on their way to market (two blocks from our house) and men en route to work in the fields or the Pemex oil refinery. Groups of men and women would stop and sit on the thick concrete sidewalks and exchange the latest gossip and jokes until loud cackles and hoots echoed through the *zaguán*.

Soon my brother-in-law Octavio's first automotive customers would arrive in their broken-down pick-ups and worn-out taxis. Octavio is a superb mechanic who always has a bevy of *chalanes* (teenage apprentices) around to help him repair cars or run errands to parts stores. For less than the price of an American tune-up he would do an expert carburetor overhaul—taking apart and carefully cleaning each of the myriad parts in gasoline—and throw in a tune-up as well. More heavy-duty jobs called for the use of his patented ramp—a thick board inclined on a rock. Unavailable parts were fashioned from wire, rubber, or other spare materials. All observations were made with the eyes and ears; no computer, oscilloscope, or other sophisticated equipment was used. The whole operation was precarious. Octavio's two small children were always climbing under cars to be next to him or sticking their hands into running engines. Miraculously, no one was injured and Octavio somehow restored the old beaters to life, including my travel-weary, Day-Glo orange, 1977 Malibu Classic station wagon.

In between clients, who were irregular at best, and during parts runs (the client usually brought the replacement parts, since Octavio had no auto parts of his own, few tools, and no shop), we sat around and shot the breeze with the gang of men who congregated every time a car hood was raised. Groups of women hovered around Margarita's store, where about one sale per hour took place, to chat. All in all, it was an ideal setting for an anthropologist to pummel the local people with ethnographic questions, an opportunity I used to full advantage.

At night, after Octavio cleaned up the puddles of oil, torn fan belts, and other debris left over from the day's work, his wife, Angelita, would open her "restaurant." She would appear with a grimy wooden table stacked with a small charcoal stove. Octavio would then light the stove with crude petroleum and Angelita would begin preparing her popular fried delicacies: tacos, tostadas, *molotes, garnachas,* and quesadillas. The food was cooked in cheap vegetable oil that was used over and over until it turned a dark brown. The various dishes were drenched in the boiling oil and served, dripping grease, with handfuls of shredded cabbage and red salsa poured over the top. I was quite familiar with Angelita's roach-infested kitchen, where she prepared the food amid swarms of flies. The dark water used to soak the cabbage was of dubious quality. Her worn cutting board was never properly cleaned. At times my stomach turned as I saw the customers wolfing down the food. At other times, washed down by a nearly frozen Coca-Cola with lime juice or a small bottle of Carta Blanca, the food was positively edible.

In any case, Angelita's little restaurant attracted a nightly gathering of diners and visitors, prey for the anthropological *preguntón.* Octavio held court next to Angelita, taking the money from the patrons and engaging in constant banter with visitors and friends. As he lounged on the two-foot-thick concrete sidewalk, his children, or sometimes the *chalanes,* would sprawl on his lap. Octavio would oblige them and occasionally play with their knees or elbows. The family across the street, composed of four unmarried adult males (and parents), also lay on the sidewalk recovering from the day's work in the corn field or a drunken binge, one man lying on the other. Casual male touching of this kind was absolutely normal and common. Many times one man would fall asleep with his head nestled on the other man's lap. The Anglo-American phobia about male-to-male physical intimacy was nowhere in evidence.

Around ten o'clock at night, Angelita's sales would wind down and the remaining stragglers would go home to sleep. This was the case most evenings, except on Saturday nights when loud dances carried on until four in the morning, fiesta nights, or on the occasion of all-night male drinking bouts. Sleeping was not always restful because of the ubiquitous biting mosquitoes and the hot, humid Isthmus air. Nocturnal scorpions and tiny black biting insects were an ever-present threat. Many a night I lay in my hammock, unable to sleep, staring up at the ceiling watching the yellow geckos (*gupayoo* in Zapotec, "the keepers of the house") studiously hunt down flies on the ceiling. Dozens of mongrel dogs would howl until someone threw a rock at them. Sometimes a *bere lele* bird (alcaravan) would unleash its plaintive wail. By five in the morning crowing roosters kick-started a new day in San Blas.

The Isthmus food took some time to get used to, but once I did I enjoyed it. Indeed, the local corn-based cuisine was one of the main reasons why my fieldwork was such a pleasant experience. Our neighbor's handmade white corn tortillas (*gueta*), cooked on a hot *comal* over a wood fire, are still the best tortillas I have eaten. The neighbor women also made a variety of *totopos* (*gueta zuquii*), the oven-baked crisp tortillas—shaped like Frisbees with lots of pinholes—that are made only in the Tehuantepec area. When I first went to the Isthmus I was unimpressed by the thin, dry, cracker-like *totopos,* but I eventually grew to love them and appreciate the fact that without any preservatives they could last for about a year without spoiling. I also came to love the various other varieties of *totopos:* sweet *totopos* (*gueta dxiña*) flavored with coconut and crude brown sugar (*piloncillo*), *gueta zuquii laga* (long thin *totopos*), *comizcalito* (round thick baked tortillas), and *gueta bi'ngui'* (round chunks of corn dough mixed with shrimp and pieces of fish and fried in oil). *Chileatole,* a hot corn gruel mixed with basil and hot chiles, was a stimulating and nutritious beverage that was particularly refreshing on the rare cool winter mornings.

The basic process for making *gueta,* the main type of tortilla consumed daily, begins the night before they are cooked. Dried corn is purchased on the cob and the kernels are stripped from the cobs and cooked for one half hour. In the morning, the cooked corn kernels are taken to the mill to be ground into *masa*. The *masa* is then mixed with lime water, and rolled and ground on a *metate* until it has the right texture and consistency. Next, a chunk of dough is torn from the mound of *masa* and rolled into a ball, then patted into a thin circular form, either on a plastic sheet which rests on a flat rock or directly in the palm of the hand. Then the raw tortilla is placed on a hot metal or clay *comal* (griddle) and cooked for about a minute or two, being turned only once. Finally the cooked tortilla is taken from the comal and placed in a large wicker basket with a towel placed on the bottom to protect the stack of tortillas and keep them warm.

The *comal* used to cook tortillas is heated by a clay oven using wood purchased from neighbors for fuel. Tortillas are made daily between nine in the morning and noon. In the afternoon, the women rest and at night they cook more corn. They do most of the work during the coolest part of the day or evening. The cooking is usually done in cramped quarters which are very hot and smoky.

Although there are poverty and malnutrition in Tehuantepec, the Isthmus Zapotecs are probably the wealthiest and best-fed indigenous people in Mexico. Their diet (except for that of the poorest peasants) is rich in proteins, carbohydrates, and vitamins. Overeating and obesity were more common than was hunger. What I especially valued, though, about local eating habits was the unbridled gusto with which people ate their food. Uninhibited by the U.S. obsession with calorie counting, nutritional guidelines, or elaborate dining etiquette, the Zapotec people I lived with chomped down their food with enthusiasm and pleasure. Dripping food on one's clothing was considered normal behavior and the occasional belch or fart evoked laughter and amusement. Eating was a hedonist's delight that was enjoyed for its own sake without the annoying drone of a television. During my fieldwork the smell of fresh bread wafting from a wood-heated clay oven in San Blas would make me salivate like Pavlov's dog.

My favorite part of Isthmus cuisine was the exquisite seafood that was cheap, abundant, and of premium quality. Most of the fish (such as *lisa, corvina,* and *mojarra*) I ate during my fieldwork was so fresh that it was never put on ice. Zapotec fishermen set their traps during the night and bring their catch to the market in the early morning. By late afternoon it has already been consumed. The Isthmus shrimp, especially the jumbo prawns, were superb, as were the other crustaceans and ocean fare such as lobster, abalone, crab, octopus, and squid. My mother-in-law's *tortas de camarón,* a kind of shrimp omelet, were to die for. After a breakfast of her *tortas de camarón* wrapped in piping hot tortillas and a cup of Oaxacan hot chocolate (a euphoric stimulant filled with alkaloids) or homegrown coffee, I could work all day without hunger. Whole red snapper fried in hot oil with abundant sliced garlic was another delicacy. Shrimp or fish soups were thoroughly healthy and delicious dishes made with chile, basil, garlic, onions, tomato, and achiote. *Cazón,* diced shark meat sauteed with garlic, onions, tomatoes, and chile, was another prized dish.

Zapotec people eat most parts of the cooked fish, including the eyes and brains. Their taste in meat is equally eclectic; little is wasted, including the cow stomach for which I never acquired a taste. The much-touted iguana meat, consumed in stews or tamales with the skin intact, was quite pleasant. Armadillo and rabbit meat, though scarce, were also flavorful. One of the most popular fiesta foods is barbecued goat or *pelibuey* (a cross between a goat and a sheep) with green salsa. Chicken basted in red *chile huajillo* and turkeys stuffed with potatoes and seasoned with mustard were delicious. *Cecina,* thin slices of pork seasoned with red chile, was greasy but satisfying when grilled over hot mesquite coals. Isthmus ways of preparing meat were clever and highly palatable. Less palatable was listening to the bleats of goats and *pelibuey* as their throats were slit in the patio in preparation for a fiesta or birthday party. But San Blas is a peasant town where domestic animals are an integral part of life.

Isthmus vegetable dishes were unremarkable, with the exception of the yellow squash and pork casserole, *chiles rellenos* made with small red *huajillo* peppers, and delicious black beans with *epazote.* The tropical fruits, however, were superior in quality. During mango season the markets were flooded with sweet green and yellow mangos of various sizes. *Chicozapotes* (sapodilas), a round thick-skinned fruit with sugary, orange flesh, was a delight. Papayas, coconuts, guanabanas, limes, and oranges were all of excellent quality. The bananas, including tiny *plátanos enanitos* and purple cooking bananas, were of a fine flavor and texture not seen in the United States. On hot afternoons, a fruit milkshake or ice-cold limeade was a marvelous thirst-quencher. I even came to like the pungent *nanches* (a sour fruit) and plums cured in alcohol that I initially found revolting.

Perhaps I belabor the flavors of the food, but if so, it is only to try to capture the feeling of being in the Isthmus. It was like a scene out of *Pedro Páramo*.[3] A gigantic, gnarled, old silk-cotton tree; the smoky smell of wood fires heating tortillas; the melancholy, nostalgic feel of an empty Isthmus street as the winter wind whipped up piles of grit and garbage; the dreamy quality of the slow-moving clouds that glided in and out of view as one gazed at them from a hammock on a sunny afternoon—these were all part of the Isthmus environment.

Throughout my fieldwork I wrestled with the sense that the mystery and romance of the Zapotec "Others" I met, the places I went, and my own experiences could not be conveyed to someone who had not been there. In recent years, anthropology has condemned essentialism and "Othering," yet who would deny that each ethnographic locale has its own ambience and texture, even if aspects of the local scene are shared with people in other places in these global times? Scrawling my impressions into my field notebook, I sometimes despaired at the thought that I could not adequately reproduce the unique idioms, meanings, and idiosyncrasies of my informants, some of whom recounted to me their exploits of sixty years ago as we drank beers and smoked cigarettes in dimly lighted bars. Putting aside the question of whether or not my informants were telling me the "truth," did I fully understand the nuances of what the person was telling me, did my notes capture the gestalt of the interview setting? Could my fieldwork account ever convey to the reader my sentiments of anxiety and hope as I stood contemplating the nature of the COCEI in Juchitán's central plaza at dusk as a fiery sunset's last rays illuminated City Hall and screeching *zanates* (crows) swarmed in the trees?

My fieldwork oscillated between periods of intense investigations of COCEI politics and the Isthmus cultural movement in Juchitán, and the more laid-back examination of Zapotec family and community dynamics in San Blas. Each aspect of the research complemented the other. Although at times living with a Zapotec family was exasperating, it was a tremendous educational experience. The first lesson I learned was that communal Indian peasant life—despite official COCEI ideology—was far from united and harmonious. Living in a close-knit Zapotec village and an even more tightly woven family, I realized that individual desires and aspirations were often frustrated by the group and that one was constantly struggling to assert one's rights and avoid the demands and obligations of others. Privacy was impossible and individualism was prohibited. The U.S. yuppie lifestle of childless self-indulgence was unheard of. The question Zapotec people ask of a person who has no children is "who will take care of you when you are old?" Isthmus people consider it indispensable to have children, especially for the later care of the elderly. Interdependence, rather than personal independence, is the social rule.

Within the Ruiz family commune there was a distinct hierarchy. The titular leader was my father-in-law, Roberto, known as *Ta Beto Soo*[4] in the Isthmus. *Ta* Beto was what I call a failed macho; that is, he was a man who aspired to be a dominant patriarch but because of his own weaknesses, illnesses, and advanced age could only bark and bellow at his family members and hope that they would obey him. *Ta* Beto's failure as a macho began with his economic decline. *Ta* Beto's father had been one of the richest men in San Blas, a rancher who pastured large herds of cattle and produced substantial crops of corn and tropical fruits on his large landholdings. He left Beto, his favorite son, an adobe house and several choice plots of agricultural land. But Beto loved the good life. A tall, handsome, charismatic man who wore a well-trimmed moustache and expensive *guayaberas,* Beto's farming activities were secondary to his fiesta-going and womanizing. Eventually, years of heavy drinking and eating made him obese and struck him with diabetes, a disease that plagues the Isthmus Zapotec people.

Beto was forced to sell the family lands and give up farming. He then took up gold jewelry making but this was hardly sufficient to provide for his seven children. Consequently, he tried to arrange a marriage between Obdulia, then a teenager, and his wealthy *compadre*. But Obdulia refused and left for Mexico City. His other daughters quickly married and left home. Soon *Ta* Beto was left with his sullen wife, angry at him for his constant pursuit of other women, and his youngest son, Octavio. Octavio, a multitalented young man, was also a bit of an underachiever, While in the third grade he quit school, despite being one of the smartest students in his class, to spend more time with his father. His elementary school teacher came to the Ruiz family home and begged him to stay in school instead of farming with his father. Octavio refused and set in motion a pattern of missed opportunities that continued throughout his life.

As a young man he was one of the best baseball players in the state of Oaxaca. He was so good that a professional team in Mexico City offered him a contract. He declined out of fear and an unwillingness to leave home. Eventually Octavio became a *chalán* in the shop of one of the best mechanics in Tehuantepec. Jovial and good-looking, he had no trouble finding female companionship, including his boss's wife. When the boss died, his widow offered Octavio half of the mechanic shop if he would manage it. Octavio declined in favor of returning home and living next door to his father, where he worked on cars in the street. Octavio's son, Robertito, became the apple of *Ta* Beto's eye and when drunk *Ta* Beto would howl about bequeathing all of his possessions to Robertito and leaving his wife and children out in the cold. Such was life at the Ruiz household.

As an outsider to the family, I tried to keep out of these conflicts as much as possible, but inevitably they would affect me. During my fieldwork things got so bad between Obdulia and her father that she chose to leave home and live with my grandmother in Wisconsin. Thus, for half of my fieldwork, I lived with her Zapotec family on my own, while she lived in the United States with my family. During that time I realized that Octavio was jealous of me because he felt that his mother, my mother-in-law, paid more attention to me than to him. On another occasion my other brother-in-law, Arturo, threw a firecracker at me, out of jealousy at my marriage to his sister. Eventually, Arturo and I became friends when I joined him in his periodic drinking binges (during which he would take a large bowl of hot chiles, eat them all, and then guzzle the juice, and other similar macho stunts).

Perhaps I have painted too dark a picture of life in Zapotec families. There were also many moments of love and affection, and long hours of laughing and joking. But life in a communal family setting was difficult at best. Togetherness meant constant intrigue and rivalries. Yet it also meant that no sick or dying person was ever left alone, and a family member always had someone to rely on. If these extended families were dysfunctional, they were certainly no more so than the average American family. At least the Ruiz family took on the challenge of living together. Many U.S. families today communicate only by long distance telephone calls or e-mail. The kinds of close interactions and sharing that breed the sort of conflicts I have mentioned are impossible in the hyper-individualized, atomistic spaces of suburban America.

The town of San Blas, like Zapotec families, is communally oriented but riven by factionalism. The center of the town's identity is the patron saint whose statue is paraded around town and celebrated each year in a noisy fiesta. The annual fiestas and the constant masses held at the church (along with the intricate and extensive kinship networks) hold the community together. The other social glue that connects the Blaseños is their sense of Zapotec Indian identity that separates them from predominantly mestizo Tehuantepec, the powerful neighboring town. Sheltered below Jaguar Hill, San Blas—along with Juchitán and a handful of other Isthmus communities—preserves much of what is left of "traditional" Zapotec culture in the Isthmus. Even today the primary language of San Blas is Zapotec.

Unlike bustling, modern Juchitán, San Blas remains a somewhat sleepy village even as it has grown to a population of roughly 20,000; and many of its residents collect televisions, video cassette players, and other symbols of modernity with a vengeance. Though large in population, San Blas—bounded by the hills, Tehuantepec River, a cemetery, and rich farm land—is extremely small in area and densely packed. House walls rub against each other. Except for the tiny town plaza, church yard, and narrow streets, there is essentially no empty space. Consequently, the dusty streets are littered with cow excrement, mango peels, and broken bottles, and are almost always filled with people or raspy *motos,* the ingenious three-wheeled vehicles that transport Blaseñas to the Tehuantepec market. Except for the hottest part of the afternoon, bands of kids play in the streets and adults lounge on the curbs. During the day, street corners are often monopolized by vendors selling sliced mangos, cucumbers, and coconuts. At night, taco stands appear. Throughout the day, and especially at night, crowds of relatives and friends sit in front of their homes and while away the hours conversing and joking. In the evening, adolescent couples hide in the shadows to make out. Aside from fiestas and church events, the public life of San Blas takes place in the streets.

Interaction between local people is so frequent that the Zapotecs have invented a clever way of acknowledging another person's existence without having to engage them in conversation. When one Zapotec person encounters another in the streets he simply says to him "*¿ma la?*" (literally "are you back or are you finished?") and the person replies "*ma*" ("yes"). This can happen a dozen times in a day without the individuals varying the routine. It is somewhat similar to the American "how ya doin?," except that in the American case there is the implied connotation that this is a question that deserves a response. In the Zapotec case it is just a way of saying "I am here" and "I recognize that you are there" without waste of time or energy in needless small talk.

Because of the density of settlement and the far-reaching strands of kinship, the average Blaseño is extremely aware of who is who in town. Anonymity is almost impossible and gossip travels as fast as lightning.[5] As they say in Mexico, "*pueblo chico, chisme grande*" ("small town, big gossip"). But there was something very democratic about San Blas street life and gossip. Every night as I sat in front of our house and chatted with my in-laws, we would criticize and make fun of passers-by and acquaintances in a comical way. Yet this was done in an egalitarian fashion in the sense that no one was immune, all were subject to attack, as we knew we were by other clusters of conversants. Since everyone's life was in the public domain, it was hard for an individual to separate himself and claim social superiority. Aspects of Blaseño social life and ethos did approximate the "closed corporate commmunity" of Wolf's typology and the shared poverty and social levelling described in the classic Mesoamerican community studies.

Transvestite gay men, *muxe's*, took part in the public culture of the San Blas streets with everyone else. The *muxe's* simply added a bit of color and flare, and they were usually not overtly discriminated against or mistreated.[6] A *muxe'* might sit down next to me and start up a flirtation or toss a *piropo* at a young man, but no one found this alarming. In this sense, the San Blas streets were very welcoming.

Under the surface, though, there were bitter currents of rivalry, struggles over land and political power, and violence. The Ruiz family, for example, never spoke to the people who lived immediately to the east of us and other neighbors and relatives could not be communicated with.[7] Worse yet, San Blas was famous for its *pistoleros* (hired gunmen). One of them, Vicente ("Chente") Sachiñas Salinas, was, conveniently, my wife's cousin, hence we were shielded from his vigilante wrath. When Chente was finally captured by the state police he was said to have killed at least thirty people (*Unomásuno* 3/13/93). His brother, Epifanio, was accused of committing eleven murders (*Extra de Oaxaca* 8/18/90). Most of these were contract killings paid for by local Istmeños involved in property or monetary disputes of some kind. One day Chente killed a friend of mine, a jovial thief we called "Puente Madera" after his hometown. I also witnessed a dead Guatemalan boy who Chente shot down in the streets after the youth attempted to steal a gold necklace from a woman at the San Blas market.

Another incident that graphically illustrated the potential for violence in San Blas occurred in 1993 when a beloved local doctor, Gaudencio Salud, was murdered by three thieves from Veracruz. The thieves were eventually captured by police and jailed in Tehuantepec. When people in San Blas heard about this a lynch mob quickly formed. The angry mob cut down the metal bars of the jail and beat the prisoners to a pulp. Subsequently, they were roped to the back of *motos* and dragged to San Blas. There they were hanged from the second story of the City Hall building, then burned with gasoline; and finally the ashy remains of their bodies were dumped along the banks of the Tehuantepec River (*El Paso Times* 2/19/93). So much for pastoral communal peasant life.

If Zapotec society was hardly a paradise, the most famous stereotype about the Isthmus—the myth of Zapotec matriarchy—was farther from the truth. As I was married to a Zapotec woman and living in a local household it became very obvious to me early in my fieldwork that Zapotec women suffered from most of the ills of patriarchy endured by women across the globe. In this respect, although I have been critical of Madison political attitudes, my training by prominent feminist scholars (especially Florencia Mallon and Ann Stoler) made it easy for me to see through the Tehuantepec Amazon mystique.[8] Indeed, one of the greatest ironies of my research was that I became the only person writing about the Isthmus regularly who criticized the notion of uniquely powerful or egalitarian Zapotec women.

The myth of Zapotec matriarchy has deep roots and is based on traveller's reports, literary works, journalistic pieces, tourist guides, local folklore, and even anthropological studies (Campbell and Green 1996). The myth exaggerates aspects of local culture such as women's control of the traditional marketplace, colorful Zapotec female attire, women's prominent role in fiestas, folklore about women controlling men with potions of *toloache* (jimson weed), and the assertive character of Isthmus women. As journalists, scholars, photographers, and writers descended on the Isthmus because of COCEI's notoriety (a minor version of the international media attention that the Zapatistas of Chiapas would later receive), I watched in astonishment as the most vulgar, sensationalist version of the Zapotec matriarchy myth began to appear on National Public Radio, and in the *New York Times, Wall Street Journal, The National Enquirer,* and even *Ms.* magazine. Especially ironic was that the intellectuals and artistic figures who propagated this myth were mostly women: Elena Poniatowska, Graciela Iturbide, a group of German anthropologists led by Veronika Bennholdt-Thomsen, and various others. I was amazed to watch the reproduction of such a simplistic and wrong-headed view of Zapotec women during a period in which feminist scholarship was revolutionizing anthropological and historical research. Yet clearly there was something compelling and thoroughly marketable about it. Why else would a television program devoted to yellow journalism like "*Ocurrió Así*" jump on the Zapotec matriarch bandwagon?

In my everyday life in a Zapotec home, I saw how countless women, including my in-laws, did battle on a daily basis with drunken, womanizing husbands. Even though I have extolled the beauty of the leisurely cantina scene, the dark side of male drinking was abandonment of the family, expenditure of scarce household resources on booze, and irresponsible, sometimes violent, behavior. In most ways, Zapotec women shared the burdens of patriarchy—the sexual double standard, double-workday, unequal access to education and employment, sexual abuse, and so on—with their sisters everywhere. Yet, the female "Zapotec-ologists," with the notable exceptions of Beverly Chiñas and Marinella Miano, were easily seduced by matriarchal folklore.

One cannot write about this matter without extolling aspects of Zapotec society that were indeed healthy for women. Clearly the culture valued women, as one saw in the fiestas, marketplace, and religious sphere where female influence was overwhelming and celebrated. The Isthmus markets were women-only spaces, as I soon learned when I began exploring them and was confronted with hoots, jeers, come-ons, and joking put-downs in the Zapotec language. Wrapped in their colorful *trajes,* striding down the streets with market baskets on their heads, or dancing at the fiestas with their heads held high, Zapotecas were proud to be women; and they shared a kind of female solidarity, a product of the sex-segregated Zapotec culture, that American women can espouse but not yet achieve.

Another irony of my fieldwork was that one way in which I could establish rapport with Zapotec male informants was through our shared experience of being "dominated" by our "matriarchal" wives. We constantly joked about the "*coscorrones*" (thumps on the head) that we received from our domineering women. This was particularly mirthful for my Juchiteco buddies, who loved the image of my diminutive wife climbing up on a *bangu'* (bench) to beat me over the head. As one of my informants, Dr. Gustavo Toledo, put it: "it is beautiful when a [Zapotec] woman dominates you, if you love her a lot." This was our motto.

As my fieldwork progressed, I began to feel more and more comfortable in the Isthmus. I loved to laze in my hammock on hot afternoons. I loved to while away the hours chatting with my friends and in-laws. I loved to drink beer in the cantinas. I loved the food. I no longer worried about the banana peels lying on the concrete floor of the house, the pig excrement in the streets, the swirling clouds of raspy dust kicked up by the Isthmus winds. I did not mind having crowds of relatives and visitors in the house at all hours of the day. I even got over my recurring stomach problems, a result of my growing immunity to local flora, rather than of my futile attempts to boil water and sanitize food. And I identified so strongly with the people and culture of San Blas that my Juchiteco friends began to call me "*el gringo de San Blas.*"

When I returned to the Isthmus after a trip back to my family home in Wisconsin, or from a research trip to Mexico City or Oaxaca City, I realized how much I appreciated the warmth of the Zapotecs. When I saw my male friends again they would smile from ear to ear and almost break my hand with the strength of their handshake, and they would not let go of my hand for several minutes. They might also put their palm on my shoulder (or in drinking situations we would sloppily embrace for several minutes) or grip my forearm. Older men would shake my hand with one hand and use the thumb and forefinger of their other hand to hold my wrist. Eventually they would release my palm from the handshake but would continue gripping my wrist for the duration of our conversation. This kind of personal affection and enthusiasm was a far cry from the frigid physical and social climate of the Germanic and Anglo-Saxon midwestern United States I came from; and it was infinitely preferable to the studied blasé attitude and ironic postures of my "postmodern" academic colleagues. For better or for worse, life in the Isthmus was passionate and intense; and I found that these emotions coincided with my worldview.

Whenever I returned to the Isthmus, one of the first things I would do was get an inexpensive massage. Massage is a common remedy for all sorts of ailments in the Isthmus, and the charge for a half-hour session was roughly four dollars. My favorite masseur was *Ta* Neto, a craggy, old, monolingual Zapotec peasant whose spry agility belied his eighty years of hard labor. *Ta* Neto gave a thorough and vigorous massage with the obligatory Vicks VapoRub (an indispensable part of the tool kit of all Isthmus masseurs and curers). Fortunately, *Ta* Neto was no longer strong enough to make the massage hurt the way "Tín Nieve," another masseur, did. Tín Nieve would jam his thumbs down on one's ligaments until one cried out in pain, and then he would push harder. I viewed it as a kind of primitive Rolfing and always dreaded the pain, although, miraculously, one never was left with lasting injuries after the massage, but simply felt relieved and rejuvenated.

As *Ta* Neto briskly rubbed my back, stomach, and legs, he would recount the exploits and malapropisms of Heliodoro Charis, the legendary Zapotec general and folk hero. Upon conclusion of the massage I would be required to rest for five or ten minutes to let my body cool off to avoid the dangerous "*aires*" (a key element of rural Mexican folklore) that could strike me down with a supernaturally derived illness if I was careless. Eventually I would get up and pay *Ta* Neto his fee. He would then wipe the sweat off his brow with the red bandanna he carried in his back pocket and gracefully waltz off.

Daily I learned about interesting Zapotec beliefs concerning illness and healing. These ranged from the bizarre to the practical: wrapping towels around the head and feet after intercourse to prevent damaging cool breezes from invading a hot body, tying a string around one's toe to prevent a cold, drinking a tall glass of lime juice the day after intercourse to prevent pregnancy, eating a lot of seafood to promote virility and fertility, drinking urine to kill various viruses, putting a child backward on a donkey and insulting him as he rides through the streets of town to overcome an illness caused by the child having seen his parents have sex,[9] and drinking chamomile and *yerbabuena* tea for just about everything.

Other remedies are based on the power of deceased individuals to return in seances and cure the ill. In San Blas many people believe that the formerly gifted Dr. Facundo Génico comes back from the dead and prescribes effective medicine to believers. One woman, I was told, suffered from a mental illness until she went to a spiritist temple in Guichevere, a barrio of Tehuantepec, and was cured by Dr. Genico's spirit. Subsequently, she became a curer herself and prescribed whatever Dr. Genico suggested to her in trances.

The spiritist temple became a popular source of medical treatments for local people. Patients included the relatives of a local woman of Arab descent (known locally as a "*Turca*") who recently died in a bus accident. The family of the dead woman went to the temple within a week after she died in order to communicate with her in seances. Obdulia's Aunt Eva also went there for treatment to cure rheumatism. She was given a treatment of herbs and other potions. When she left the temple after the treatments, the sun burned her skin severely during the time it took her to cross the street and walk about a block. Another cure she received consisted of applying petroleum and alcohol to her knee and binding it with a wrap, which again burned her skin badly. Despite the harsh side effects of these treatments, Eva felt they improved her rheumatic condition, although she said she was getting tired of unorthodox treatments. Nonetheless, she scoffed at conventional medical approaches that involve taking pills, which she derisively called *chuchitos*.[10] Eva believed strongly in spirits and local healing methods.

My most personal experience with Zapotec curing methods occurred after I suffered a sharp kink in my neck from long hours of typing my first paper for publication on my research in Mexico. My mother-in-law, Elvira, heard me complaining about neck pain when I came to breakfast in the morning. She immediately diagnosed the problem as the "evil eye" and prescribed a ritual cleansing (*limpia*). Elvira said that a beautiful woman had stared at me when I went to market in Tehuantepec the other day. Her desire for me, expressed through her eyes, was what had caused my neck ailment. The *limpia* consisted of my mother-in-law vigorously rubbing Vicks VapoRub on my shoulder while spitting alcohol onto me as she repeated a series of incantations. As I recall it now, her chants were something to the effect of "go away evil spirits, go away devil, go away you pig," and so on. She proceeded to rub and beat my back, head, and shoulders with a bouquet of aromatic basil leaves. She also pounded on my neck and ears with her hands. After about fifteen minutes of this, she was done and I was "cured." The next morning when I woke up my neck pain was gone but my ear was painful and swollen. When I reported this to my mother-in-law she was devastated and attributed my problems to my lack of faith in her methods.

Although I still was not a 100 percent Istmeño, Elvira had enough trust in me at a later date to send me to pick *toloache* leaves for her to use as a poultice on her achy, arthritic knees. According to local folklore, which reflects the mythology of Zapotec matriarchy, *toloache* (jimson weed) leaves are ground up by Zapotec women and put in their men's food in order to make them zombies and to control them sexually. I had second thoughts as I collected those leaves.

My ambivalence about Zapotec folk beliefs would recur on numerous occasions, especially after Obdulia and I adopted her sister's child in 1994. The baby (now my daughter, Ruth) was born prematurely and was in very delicate health at the beginning. From the hospital we took our one-month-old infant home to the steamy heat of our brick and concrete dwelling. Despite the crushing Isthmus temperatures and humidity, my female in-laws insisted on bundling and swaddling our sweaty child. I had tremendous fears about the baby becoming dehydrated and seriously ill and suggested she be placed in a room with a strong cooling fan. This idea was immediately vetoed, much to my dismay.

In this instance, as on many other occasions, I found myself wondering about the anthropological notion of cultural relativism that we glibly teach our students. According to this basic anthropological doctrine, all cultural values and beliefs are essentially equally valid. In the interest of avoiding ethnocentrism, we must, according to this perspective, not pass judgment on other people's customs and ways of life. But at a number of times during my fieldwork I found myself thinking that the Zapotec culture is rich and creative, but I would rather do things the way I had been taught back home.

As I became more accustomed and assimilated to life in the Isthmus, I began to realize the banality of some current theoretical obsessions in American cultural anthropology. One of these that was at its peak during the 1980s was the critique of the concept of tradition. Unleashed by Hobsbawm's brilliant formulation of the "invention of tradition," the stylish way of thinking became to view with skepticism any cultural element considered traditional and to brand as essentialist anyone who argued for cultural continuity or permanence (Hobsbawm and Ranger 1983). How would Blaseños, who live in a town that is at least 500 years old, view such an idea? Was their town just a cultural construction, an imagined community? Were the tasty tortillas that they have been eating, according to their perspective, since "time immemorial," a creative fiction? Were their customs really recent inventions of crafty powerbrokers?

Another set of trendy ideas that was rich in possibilities, but overused and overextended, was Clifford's celebration of cultural pastiche and fragmented postmodern identities (Clifford 1988). From this standpoint, the old anthropological narrative about disappearing cultures and the need for salvage ethnography was irrelevant in the modern or postmodern world. In Clifford's view, all claims to cultural authenticity were suspect and essentially a discourse, especially in the postmodern, transcultural world of emergent cultural mixture and hybridity. Clifford's powerful critique of older essentialist models of culture and his call for a new ethnography of the rapidly crisscrossing and multiplying cultural identities in the current era was salutary and enlightening. In the wrong hands, however, the obsession with emergent culture and the disdain for "essentialist" notions could lead to a theoretical dead-end for anthropology. Specifically, it could prevent us—in our zeal to discover new cultural forms—from recognizing the obvious, that is, that the loss of languages, customs, and indeed entire cultures is often an irreversible tragedy for which no amount of playful cultural pastiche can compensate.

These ideas occurred to me as I rested in my hammock gazing at the plumes of acrid smoke billowing from the Salina Cruz PEMEX refinery. For me it was obvious that the helter-skelter economic growth and "development" transforming the Isthmus was a direct threat to the survival of the Isthmus Zapotec culture.[11] Yes, development meant that more money was channelled into the *velas,* now videotaped and announced on the radio; a Zapotec radio station (*Radio Teca*) was created; more expensive *huipiles* and gold filagree jewelry were purchased; and some Zapotecs drove cars and trucks. But it also meant that iguanas had to be "imported" from other regions to meet Isthmus culinary (and symbolic) needs, turtle eggs became scarce and endangered, the ocean and Isthmus lagoons were polluted with oil and gas spills, noisy *motos* and trucks clogged the narrow village streets and destroyed peace and quiet, and so on, ad infinitum. It meant that young Istmeños often learned only the Spanish language, and their conversations were filled with soap opera trivia, American video-movie dialogue, and baseball statistics, instead of puns in the Zapotec language, discussion of Isthmus history and folklore, or the telling of *cuentos* (folktales) and "lies" (*guenda rusiguii*), a genre of Isthmus story-telling. Urbanization, the destruction of agricultural lands, and industrial development in the Isthmus were truly, to invoke Joni Mitchell, the paving of paradise to put up a parking lot. Postmodern cultural irony can not make up for this loss.

In this age of global travel, cultural homogenization, and rampant consumerism, I still see great value in the village way of life that San Blas typifies but is quickly losing. "*Los Esquineros,*" a gang of neighborhood kids who eventually formed their own soccer team, spent countless hours camped out on a concrete curb on one corner of Hidalgo Street near our house, endlessly engaged in the playful games, jokes, and rituals of youth. There will be little time or space for this behavior—conducted primarily in the Zapotec language—in the twenty-first century if the current mindless pursuit of consumer items, full-time industrial jobs, and the proliferation of cars and trucks that make casual lounging on curbs dangerous, continues. Will the resounding laughs and clapping of gossipping crowds of Zapotec women be replaced by the hum of air conditioners and washing machines? Will the hard, crumbly white cheese from Chiapas (that I used to say smelled like dirty feet until I took a liking to it), the dried shrimp, and *totopos* that Istmeños ritually take with them on bus trips to other regions—as a tangible symbol of their Isthmus identity—be replaced by Pan Bimbo, Sabritas, and Big Macs?

The more I explored the Isthmus towns, the more enamored I became of specific street corners, alleys, shaded park benches in the Tehuantepec Plaza, and nooks and crannies under the arches of Juchitán City Hall. The particular spaces and places of the Isthmus, the riotously odoriferous markets, churches smelling of spicy incense and sweet flowers, the lurid colors of Isthmus fiesta *trajes* and procession banners, the sounds of firecrackers exploding after weddings, the lyrics of Isthmus *sones,* the nasal sing-song rhythms of conversations in the Zapotec language—all of this was part of the exhuberant cultural life that economic development and cultural change threatens, and that trendy anthropological theories could reduce to inventions, indigenous essentialism, or mere constructions. This unique Zapotec way of living was also COCEI's cultural identity, and its defense a main plank in the movement's political platform.

As my fieldwork progressed, I also came to love the Isthmus land and sea. Oaxaca is blessed with some of the most beautiful, wild beaches in the Western Hemisphere. Despite the construction of the new tourist complex in Huatulco, many of these beaches remain undeveloped paradises for swimming, sunbathing, and beer drinking. I am especially fond of the little beach *fondas*—ramshackle restaurant huts built of *carrizo*, driftwood, and palm leaves—constructed by Zapotec entrepreneurs who sell delicious fresh fish and shrimp cooked with chile and garlic and served with ice-cold beer. These windswept joints, whose furniture consists of little more than a few stringy, frayed hammocks and wooden tables and chairs, have the romantic feel of a gypsy camp or pirate compound. The combination of blue ocean, bright sunshine, cool breezes along the Isthmus shore, and the rocky crags and windswept Isthmus tropical fruit trees and battered corn plants, provides a stunning backdrop. This colorful tableau is accentuated by traditionally dressed Huave and Zapotec women who cruise by with baskets of shrimp, *gueta bi'ngui'*, and *quesadillas de elote* on their heads.

I also cherish the quirky beauty of the Isthmus farmland and rural areas. The tall, spindly coconut palms, the bushy overloaded mango trees pregnant with fruit, the exotic *chicozapote,* and hardy banana plants. Gnarled mesquite and spiny *huizache*, organ-shaped pitayas, giant silk-cotton trees with branches reaching out almost horizontal to the ground, and the perfumed flowers of *guie' chaachi,* jasmine, and frangipani. The dessicated, xerophytic look of the Isthmus during the perennial droughts and rainless winter season. The eruption of tropical smells after a summer rain. The fronded oasis of Laollaga and its sweet natural spring water. The rugged badlands and dusty byroads to Colonia Alvaro Obregón, Monte Grande, and Unión Hidalgo filled with bandits and thieves. The carefully tended plots of dwarf-like *zapalote* corn surrounded by fifty-feet-tall coconut palms, tamarinds, and tropical fruits of all varieties. A peasant farmer plowing his field with oxen. Herds of goats and *pelibueyes* tended by young kids with sticks to keep them in line. Humble farm houses made of crooked poles and palm thatch roofs, adobe and wattle-and-daub, or *carrizo* cane. The inevitable gusts of Tehuantepec wind. The tropical birds and buzzing of insects. Occasionally, the slither of an endangered iguana. This was the place I came to love. My romantic attachment to the place and its people did not fit the ironic postmodern mood then sweeping the U.S. academy.

My passion for the Isthmus grew as I strengthened my ties with my in-laws and neighbors. I became a *padrino* (godfather) for twin *quinceañeras* and I attended many weddings and birthday parties. I went to numerous fiestas and drank beer in countless cantinas and house parties. I gave numerous gifts of money, beer, clothing, painting supplies, books, and a typewriter to my COCEI informants. I constantly transported friends and acquaintances in my Malibu station wagon; on one occasion I overloaded the car with so many heavy-weight Tehuanas that the car's tires scraped against the wheel well. For better or worse, my fieldwork was fueled by passion: passion for my wife and her family, passion for my local friends, and love of the Zapotec culture and the Isthmus landscape. Some researchers jump conveniently from country to country chasing trendy research topics and a stylish lifestyle with juicy grant money. I did not have that option, nor did I desire it.

Eventually I found myself identifying strongly with Isthmus people, especially the Blaseños and Juchitecos. I began to speak like them: in Juchitán, people said I pronounced Zapotec words like a Blaseño and Juchitecos would refer to San Blas as my pueblo. Sometimes the Juchitecos would say I was from Tehuantepec, I would feign annoyance and correct them by saying, "No, I am from San Blas." I would remind them that San Blas was a rebellious town like Juchitán. I dressed like the locals with my colored *guayaberas,* jeans, and huaraches.

I felt especially close to the Istmeños at parties held at the Ruiz family compound. Typically there would be two large stew pots of barbecued *pelibuey* and vast amounts of beer. Most invited guests would come, including numerous San Blas neighbors, several families of in-laws, and friends from Juchitán and Tehuantepec. Another poignant moment was the death of Ernesto, a *muxe'* neighbor. Ernesto, Neto for short (I never knew his full name), was universally beloved in our San Blas neighborhood. He was the most feminine *muxe'* I ever met, and he had a smooth, delicate way of dressing and conversing—heightened by an exaggerated campiness—that was loved by everyone. As he passed by on the street, he had a kind word for each neighbor, and a subtle come-on or sexual joke for the young men. With a laugh and a comically limp-wristed wave, he was on his way.

Neto liked to drink and party. While drunk one night, he wandered onto the Trans-Isthmus highway and was killed by a *moto*. The news spread quickly to San Blas. Soon Neto's relatives were scurrying around to make arrangements to deal with his corpse. The horror, sadness, and anxiety provoked by Neto's death was etched in the faces of his relatives. Neighbors—men and women alike—were soon sitting or standing in front of their houses weeping. The wake was held the night of his death in Neto's *carrizo* hut a short distance up the alley from our house. All night long I listened to the haunting dirges of the funeral music and the plaintive wails of Neto's relatives: "Why are you leaving us, don't go away, aaay, Neto . . . nooo." I will never forget the pathetic look on his cousin Miguel's face as tears streamed and the brass band droned out "La Llorona," "Dios Nunca Muere," and other regional tunes. It was a sad night that we all shared.

Despite my recurrent bouts of diarrhea and insomnia (my bedroom was a small sauna-like brick room that made sleeping difficult), frequent hangovers, and anxiety about the success of my fieldwork and the dangers of studying radical politics in Mexico, Isthmus life was becoming my own. Near the end of my research, feelings of nostalgia and romanticism surfaced in my fieldnotes:

How interesting and yet how melancholy it has been for me to return to the Isthmus. It is now so easy for me to adapt to this way of life; it is like putting on a pair of comfortable, worn shoes. So different it is for me now than when I first came and suffered from the heat, strange customs, staring eyes of children, and the foreign environment. Now this is no longer new—I feel like I understand the society and how it functions and I know many people and my way around town.

It is sad to see old people dying and babies now becoming teenagers or teenagers married with children. To see such drastic changes in the lives of the townspeople and the physical features of the community makes me wonder at how fast time has flown, and it makes me sad to think how little time I am able to spend here because of my job in the U.S.

Yet I am glad to be here at least for a short time to marvel at the way family and social relations dominate life, to observe the ruggedly handsome, antiquated yet still functional *carretas* (oxcarts); the dynamism, zest, and color of the women; the picturesque *carrizo,* adobe and brick homes with worn wooden beams and crumbling bricks; the endless playing of children without any purpose but glee; the tireless joking of the men—doing what their parents did. This all seems so timeless, as if in San Blas time stood still even though the rapid economic developments belie this.

As I walked around San Blas with Tío Víctor, Robertito, and Pedro during three different walks I was again struck by the red tile roofs; dirty gravel streets with pieces of brick and feces; spiny green and brown vegetation—mesquite, *huizache*, and creosote; and the swaying palms of the Isthmus. These images will always stay with me, as well as the images of winding, rocky streets and steep *callejones* of San Blas—the unusual angles these sometimes take in order to adapt to the homes of the people—the languid pace of life, the screeching birds at dusk, the tired *mancuernas* (ox-teams) bringing the wooden oxcarts home in the evening, the stacks of cornstalks in front of people's *solares*, the creative disorder of possessions strewn all over the place in people's homes; the pigs and dogs rooting around the streets, squealing, and running off.

For about half of my fieldwork, Obdulia was with me in the Isthmus. She accompanied me several days a week on outings to Juchitán and elsewhere. At times she translated Zapotec words for me or provided other clarifying information. My debt to her for her help with the research is enormous. Much of my knowledge and understanding of Zapotec women's lives comes from what she told me about her own life and personal experiences in the Isthmus. She has written about this as well (Ruiz Campbell 1993). Yet much of my research was also a solitary pursuit in Juchitán while she attended to family affairs in San Blas (and later returned to Madison). In any case, I feel that only Obdulia can tell her story and her feelings about being involved in an anthropological research project; it would be presumptuous of me to attempt it.

Living with a Zapotec family in San Blas gave me deep insight into local beliefs and customs. It also helped me establish an identity as an insider in the Isthmus. These advantages did not immediately translate into effective research on radical politics. Gaining inside access to the controversial COCEI political movement was a long, slow process marked by breakthroughs and setbacks.

NOTES

1. "*Butaque*" is a Zapotecized spelling of the Spanish "*butaca.*"

2. Isthmus people often refer to the act of manipulating someone or tricking them (often through flattery) as "*jugandole la cabeza,*" literally "playing with his (or her) head."

3. A classic surrealist novel by the great Mexican writer Juan Rulfo.

4. *Ta Beto Soo* literally means "tall Mr. Roberto" in Zapotec. "*Ta*" is the Zapotec equivalent of "*Señor*" in Spanish; *Soo* means "tall." In Isthmus towns, most people are known by their nicknames and only secondarily by their full, legal names.

5. A good example of this occurred one afternoon when I went to Salina Cruz to go swimming in the ocean. En route I stopped to eat some watermelon to quench my thirst during the hot afternoon. The next day I suffered

from acute diarrhea. When some friends came to visit I told them I was sick, and they said "Oh, yes, that is because you ate watermelon yesterday when your body was hot from the sun, we saw you." Everywhere I went during my fieldwork townspeople observed my actions. Later they would report to me that they had seen me in a certain cantina, at the market, and so on.

6. For a more critical discussion of ways in which Zapotec *muxe's* are treated unequally, see Campbell (1994, 238–239).

7. Bickering with neighbors sometimes led to fistfights or shouting matches. More commonly, however, it consisted of everyday forms of harassment such as when my mother-in-law placed chunks of broken glass in the alley by our house in order to prevent the neighbors (who did not have an indoor bathroom) from urinating against the wall.

8. I do not dwell on this issue here because Obdulia and I have addressed it at length elsewhere (see Campbell and Green 1996; also Ruiz Campbell 1993).

9. This illness is known locally in Spanish as *pegatriste* and in Zapotec as *dxibi guidxa*.

10. Pills of little effectiveness.

11. Compare this view to that of Rubin (1997) who argues that the refinery and other economic developments of this kind, rather than threatening peasant survival, simply made farmers into proletarians. If the balance of Isthmus ecology is completely destroyed by rampant development and the Isthmus becomes almost exclusively urban, no doubt Zapotec culture will survive but it will surely have lost much of what made it unique and so appealing to hundreds of journalists, artists, social scientists, and, of course, the Zapotec people themselves.

Isthmus of Tehuantepec

San Blas market

Alley in San Blas, Ruiz family home on right

San Blas street scene

Miguel and ox-team, San Blas

Chela making tortillas

Shrimp in Juchitán market

Muxe' in San Blas

Oscar Martínez, Isthmus painter

Juchitán Cultural Center

Rock art painting by Israel Vicente

San Vicente Ferrer Church in Juchitán

COCEI political demonstration, 1988

Juchitán City Hall

Coceístas

Zapotec musician Heber Rasgado, painter Israel Vicente, and the author
in El Paso, Texas

Ruth Campbell wearing a *traje tehuana*

Obdulia Campbell, Howard Campbell, Sonia Godoy, and
Elvira Ruiz

CHAPTER 4

COCEI Radical Politics

My research grants and connections with prominent academics in Mexico City were a good starting point for my project, but the success of my research hinged on establishing positive relations with the COCEI leaders and intellectuals in Juchitán. My first key COCEI informant, Manuel López Mateos, was a longtime friend of the distinguished Mexican sociologist Sergio Zermeño. When I talked with Zermeño in the capital, he said that when I got to Juchitán I had to speak with López Mateos, who was married to a member of one of the most powerful and conservative Zapotec business and political families in a kind of Romeo and Juliet relationship. López Mateos was a mathematics professor at UNAM and former director of COCEI's radical radio station, *Radio Ayuntamiento Popular.* Libia, his wife, was the daughter of a former PRI mayor of Juchitán, and several of her brothers and sisters were married into conservative PRI political families.

Libia and Manuel lived in Libia's mother's barracks-like home (reminiscent of Pancho Villa's house in Chihuahua, Chihuahua) in the center of Juchitán, close to the mother's hardware store. The mother, *Na*[1] Manuela, was a classic Zapotec female powerhouse who spoke little Spanish but ran her business and family with an iron will. Still active in her seventies, *Na* Manuela was an impressive figure as she hustled about decked out in her colorful Isthmus blouse and billowing petticoats. López Mateos, on leave from UNAM, eked out a precarious existence as a math textbook translator amid the suspicion and hostilities of his *priísta* in-laws who viewed him as a radical leftist and an urban egghead to boot. Even though his father was from Juchitán, Manuel grew up in Mexico City and learned little of the Zapotec language.

Anthropological instincts told me he was an ideal informant: an articulate but knowledgeable insider who was also a marginal man with a desire to tell his story to the outside world. López Mateos had studied at the University of Wisconsin, my alma mater. Furthermore, my father and López Mateos were mathematicians, so we shared more common ground. Initial interactions were smooth and alcohol-lubricated. We talked about Isthmus society and politics. We drank long into the night, slapping each other on the back and laughing. Manuel and Libia invited Obdulia and me to several *velas*, and as an invited guest of prominent Juchitecos I began to expand my connections. But I soon realized that López Mateos had limited potential for me as an informant. Perhaps the problem was that we were too alike or maybe that he (already a university professor and well-versed in the Zapotec culture) was in the driver's seat and I was his passenger. Whatever the case, after a certain point in the relationship I realized that Manuel and I had reached an impasse.

I suppose Manuel saw me as someone fresh out of Madison with research money to burn, but somewhat wet behind the ears and still a novice in the ways of Juchitán and the COCEI. It finally occurred to me that Manuel probably viewed me as an intellectual competitor, something I hardly expected as a young, unestablished researcher. After considerable hospitality on his part, our amiable late-night discussions disintegrated into intellectual combat. His offers to connect me with COCEI leaders, with the exception of Oscar Cruz, never materialized. The low ebb of this relationship came one night in a dingy cantina when I found myself stone drunk, buying beer, but learning nothing about my research topic and feeling frustrated. I realized I had to pursue other options.

Fortunately, one night at Manuel's house, Oscar Cruz, one of the then up-and-coming young leaders of the COCEI, paid Manuel a visit. After a period of initial mistrust, Cruz and I became firm friends and from then on I had direct access to the COCEI leadership without brokerage. I still had been unable to interview the three main COCEI leaders (Héctor Sánchez, Polín, and Daniel López Nelio). This unfinished business became an obsession. Yet the more I tried, the harder it became. I would arrange interviews through intermediaries (such as

Polín's sister) and the leader would not show up. People would offer to put me in contact with the COCEI politicians but they would not follow through. Eventually I realized that interviewing the leadership was, for the moment at least, a dead-end, and this liberated me to seek other avenues for understanding the COCEI political movement.

The doors to the Juchitán Cultural Center were always open and I took advantage of this to devour their holdings of books, magazines, and theses concerned with the Isthmus. There was much material there that was relevant to COCEI and the Zapotec cultural movement. I began to learn how COCEI emerged in the 1970s as a political movement of disgruntled Zapotec students, disenfranchised peasants, and poor workers. I read about COCEI's astonishing victory in Juchitán mayoral elections in 1981 and its subsequent bloody ouster from office by the Mexican military. I followed COCEI's years of martyrdom and victimization by PRI *pistoleros* and soldiers, and studied how the movement's struggle for democracy gained international recognition. I absorbed the story of COCEI eventually regaining political control of Juchitán and becoming one of the few cities in Mexico ruled by leftist Indians.

COCEI's ethnic dimension was especially interesting to an anthropologist. Juchitán has a remarkable history of political and military conflicts that can be traced back to the Zapotec conquest of the Isthmus in the fourteenth century. At that time, Zapotecs took the best Isthmus land from the Huave and Mixe Indians and established settlements in what became Juchitán, Tehuantepec, and San Blas. According to Juchiteco folklore, the most formidable Zapotec warriors founded the town of Juchitán on the inhospitable, wind-swept plains and the rugged conditions there further toughened the character of Juchitán residents (Henestrosa 1993). Isthmus Zapotec fought several wars with the Aztecs who were never able to establish complete hegemony in the region (Campbell 1994).

After the Spanish Conquest, Zapotecs engaged in a series of battles that sharpened their sense of ethnic distinction and pride. One key episode was the Tehuantepec Rebellion of 1660 in which Zapotecs overthrew Spanish authorities and controlled their town for one year. Other important historical events include the Battle of September 5, 1866 (in which Juchiteco townspeople successfully defended their town against a small troop of pro-Maximilian French soldiers) and the Che Gómez Rebellion in Juchitán during the Mexican Revolution. All of these incidents became part of a Juchiteco Zapotec self-concept of ethnic pride, if not arrogance.

Zapotec notions of separateness are based on an origin myth that the Zapotecs are the "cloud people" (*binniza*) who descended to Oaxacan soil from the heavens. Zapotecs see themselves as different from (if not superior to) all other types of people who are called, somewhat derisively, *dxu'* in the native language. COCEI leaders framed their contemporary political struggles with the PRI, and for control of land, local resources, and municipal power, in terms of a glorious struggle by Zapotecs for freedom from exploitation by *dxu'* in Oaxaca City and Mexico City. These ideas also became key themes of the Zapotec writers, painters, and musicians who tirelessly extolled the beauty of their culture and the righteousness of the COCEI political struggle in books, paintings, and songs.

Getting inside such an ethnically conscious political and cultural movement was the main challenge of my fieldwork. Luckily, I established strong rapport with Macario Matus, the director of the Juchitán Cultural Center, and he became my key informant and drinking partner. I met dozens of fascinating bohemian artists, musicians, and writers who became my best friends in Juchitán and provided me with vast amounts of information about COCEI's history and organization. Many of the artists and their friends were also *coceístas*, so little by little I built a broad base of buddies, contacts, and acquaintances among the middle level cadre of COCEI activists and intellectuals.

One, a sociologist, told me he would gladly discuss COCEI politics with me but he would not submit to a questionnaire. From then on I no longer confronted interviewees with written questions and, for the most part, I did not use a tape recorder, because of the delicate nature of my research. I memorized a series of question and interview topics and produced them verbally when opportunities arose. Most of my interviews took place in informal settings: bars, *velas*, visits to friends' homes, COCEI political demonstrations, birthday parties, and beer-drinking gatherings. I was always on the alert for information about COCEI and memorized what I learned, then wrote it in my notebook at the first opportunity—usually out of the view of the people around me. It was not until near the end of my fieldwork that I felt comfortable that I would not be harassed by Mexican political spies or distrustful COCEI adherents.

There were a number of frightening incidents in which my role as anthropologist was challenged. One night in the Bar Jardín, a drunken bodyguard of Mario Bustillo, the most powerful PRI cacique, confronted me over and over with the question of "*¿que pretendes, aqui?*" ("What are you trying to do here?") until I was finally rescued by the bar owner, Julio Bustillo, ironically the son of the cacique. On another occasion, I was caught in Juchitán after midnight and there were no more buses to take me back home to Tehuantepec. That day I had cashed my fellowship check at a Juchitán bank and I was carrying all of my money (900,000 pesos) for the month, along with my invaluable field notebook chock full of fresh information. Half drunk and desperate to get home I unwisely hitchhiked a ride with a Oaxaca state military truck full of the hated "*azules*," blue-uniformed soldiers famous for repressing COCEI protests. As I sat in the bed of the truck with a dozen soldiers I clutched my briefcase and morbidly imagined how easy it would be for them to simply take my money and leave me in a field alongside the Pan-American Highway or, worse yet, knock me on the head with a rifle butt. Thankfully, none of this happened, and I gave the officer in charge a firm handshake as he dropped me off.

There were other disturbing incidents. On one occasion, I was drinking with some Juchiteco painters in a bar called El Carrusel when we were joined by several upper-level COCEI leaders (members of the approximately sixteen-member junta known as the *Dirección Política* that makes most of the key decisions about COCEI policy). Things seemed to be going well as we downed numerous Coronas until a rugged, scar-faced bodyguard known as "Panza" (who turned out to be a jovial character I later considered a friend) turned to me and told me that the COCEI knew that I was prying into their affairs, that I was a spy. I acted as if he was joking and continued with the barroom revelry, but inside I was trembling. As time went by I saw that Panza and his bosses were no threat to me and that he was just testing me, but it was a delicate moment. As I learned more about COCEI I realized that the leadership's reluctance to talk to me was based on the fact that about thirty *coceístas* have been murdered by their *priísta* enemies or Mexican government agents, and that hundreds of COCEI members have been jailed as a result of political repression. Their caution and suspicion of outsiders was justified and legitimate.

Another difficult encounter at the beginning of my fieldwork involved a hanger-on to the Zapotec cultural scene (ironically named Carlos Fuentes, the same name as one of Mexico's most famous intellectuals). Fuentes began probing me about my research and finally stated flatly that I was not needed because the Zapotecs already had their own intellectuals who successfully studied their history and culture. I weakly replied that I thought I could at least disseminate this history in the United States, but that in any case I had a right to be there because I was married to a Zapotec woman. Finally, Carlos's drinking companions calmed him down, and on a later occasion he apologized for his aggressiveness. We ultimately became friends and I used to jokingly refer to him as Octavio Paz.

At a fiesta early in my fieldwork, I met a sharply dressed man, hiding behind shiny sunglasses, who I was later told was a government informer. And on a regular basis I would watch the San Blas *pistolero*'s heavily armed bodyguards patrolling the streets in their sinister-looking white Topaz. Other moments, though less intimidating, could be equally discouraging. At times I felt like some kind of Viking invader, standing alone at COCEI demonstrations. There were many nights that I rang up big bills at Ramon Bragaña's funky palm-thatched restaurant waiting for interviewees who never showed up, or just hoping that someone interesting would happen along. Other late nights, thoroughly inebriated from long afternoons and evenings of drinking with uncooperative informants, I wondered what the hell I was doing as I flew down the bumpy, potholed lawless road—with a sheer drop-off on either side—that connected Juchitán and Tehuantepec. Was I ruining my health and engaging in a dangerous lifestyle for the sake of rapport, and then not even achieving that? These were the anxieties that plagued me in my darker moments. My frustrations even boiled over with COCEI leader Polín's wife when I called to confirm an interview which he had already cancelled numerous times. When she said "no, he is not available," I blew up and told her that I did not care, that it did not matter to me anyway.

This anger was productive, however, because it caused me to face reality. Not everyone wants to be interviewed by a gringo anthropologist. Clearly, my best approach was to become part of the woodwork and blend into the COCEI by osmosis. I also pursued other research angles such as the archives of the Tehuantepec Cultural Center, and various newspaper collections. Eschewing a frontal assault on the COCEI leaders, I decided to also interview leaders of the local PRI (the political party that ruled Mexico for seventy-one years), the bitter enemies of COCEI.

My first major PRI interview was with the suave young mayor of Juchitán. He, like a number of Juchiteco politicians, was a sociologist, and had already published a book about politics in Juchitán. The book,

El Crepúsculo del Poder, contained useful insights and analyses of Isthmus politics but was marred by his clumsy use of pseudonyms. In a town where everyone knows everyone's business, and political leaders are always in the spotlight, the mayor chose pseudonyms like "Leocadio de Gide" for Leopoldo de Gyves and "Nestor Vianchez" for Héctor Sánchez; this fooled few of the readers of the book. Nonetheless, I was nervous as I interviewed him. I knew that the PRI mayor would mistrust me and assume that, like most other researchers attracted to Juchitán, I was supportive of the radical COCEI movement. No doubt he had already heard that I had been hanging out in bars with *coceístas*.

It was the beginning of my fieldwork and here I was dealing with a smooth, accomplished politician who had conducted scholarly research on the topic I was pursuing and was, moreover, a native of the community and thoroughly versed in its customs and history. As I sat in the mayor's spartan office in Juchitán's historic City Hall building (site of COCEI's controversial five-month sit-in protest and subsequent ouster by the Mexican military in 1993) gazing at the framed pictures of Benito Juárez and Heliodoro Charis, famous Oaxacan politicians, I was in awe of how quickly I had gained access to the local political scene that obsessed my imagination. I was also overawed by the slick *priísta* and I pondered the irony that this young man was the wealthy mayor of his home town and the father of two children, while I was still a graduate student (with no children) doing my thesis.

In this context, surrounded by PRI henchmen and bodyguards, I decided that the best strategy was to be humble and let the scholar-politician do most of the talking. I asked him questions that gave him a chance to persuade me that the COCEI movement was, in fact, the bad guys, not the PRI. The strategy worked to perfection. In the mayor's office and over a long, leisurely seafood lunch at a fine local restaurant (the bill paid for by City Hall), I received the most sophisticated version of Juchiteco PRI ideology, that is, that Isthmus Zapotec cultural revivalism and the Juchiteco ethnic political struggle were not the sole provinces of COCEI, that the PRI was also taking up these causes but doing it in a modern, noncombative way.

Naturally, I was skeptical of the *priísta* viewpoint, however shrewdly worded, and I continued to view that party as a bastion of corruption. This perspective was reinforced by a key comment made to me by a leading Juchiteco *priísta*. In response to my question about whether there was still corruption in Juchitán now that the PRI had modernized local politics, the *priísta* knowingly replied, "but of course there still are ways of stealing government money . . . if not, then why go into politics in the first place?"

If the mayor represented the reform-oriented, moderate branch of the local PRI, its backward, cynical wing was embodied in the person of my wife's relative, whom I will call "Lalo." I met Lalo at my in-law's family gatherings but when I came to the Isthmus to do fieldwork our interactions increased. Lalo was a low-level functionary of the PRI regional office in the Isthmus. His job was to do the errands and dirty work required to keep the PRI in power. He was essentially a go-between, what in Mexico is referred to as a *coyote* or an *achichincle.* Lalo was thoroughly corrupt, he would do anything for a price, and everyone knew it; he displayed his hunger for power and money with every word and gesture. He bragged that he could fix elections. He would scheme openly and discuss his recent *transas* (corrupt dealings). Lalo was viewed with disdain by many of his relatives, and his father-in-law openly criticized his Machiavellian attitude in my presence.

Yet Lalo was family, so they put up with him. When he found out I had a car he began to call me and say, "Come and pick me up, I have some important information to tell you about Isthmus politics." I would dutifully pick him up and he would toss me some bit of useless political trivia and demand to be taken to Juchitán. On one occasion I drove him to the offices of a local newspaper so that he could deliver a bribe (*chayote*) to the editor to ensure a PRI spin on a story about recent political events. In addition to demanding my services as a chauffeur, Lalo also began to pump me about my research, what I was studying and why, what my conclusions were, and what COCEI was planning. As I became more savvy in the ways of the Isthmus I learned to promise him a lot and produce almost nothing. I gave him a few articles and papers unrelated to what I was really doing and he, in turn, gave me a few notecards with brief descriptions of Juchiteco politicians that were of little value. But I did make some valuable contacts through Lalo, and I gained insight into the realities of realpolitik, Zapotec-style.

My other contacts with *priísta* politicians were equally instructive. From the most traditional Isthmus cacique, I learned that old-guard PRI power was based on local clientelism, political alliances, and brokerage with regional and national political forces, not necessarily on charisma or ideological sophistication, as in the case of the young mayor. The inarticulate cacique barely understood my research questions and responded with mumbled monosyllables and grunts. He was virtually useless as an informant; however, it was fascinating to be in the home of a powerful regional boss. Although the cacique adroitly manipulated Zapotec customs (such as fiesta sponsorship) and kinship ties, he did it in an absolutely unconscious way, without the overt ethnic political ideology wielded by COCEI or PRI moderates. He was truly a "dinosaur" (old-style Mexican politician) in the full sense of the word.

During this period I interviewed other PRI politicians, including César Augusto Carrasco, a polished government bureaucrat and former mayor of Juchitán. I discussed local politics with Mario López, a prominent businessman and gifted guitar player. López was interesting because he was of the same generation as the COCEI leaders and had been involved in the early phases of the movement before switching to the PRI. Although he lived a comfortable lifestyle in a California-style mansion in a new upper-class suburban neighborhood removed from the gritty, earthy street life of central Juchitán, he was steeped in Zapotec folklore and was one of the most gifted Zapotec singer/songwriters. López and Carrasco clearly showed me that Zapotec history and culture were not only defended and promoted by leftist *coceístas* but were the common heritage that all Juchitecos shared and exploited politically, even though COCEI was much more adept at this than was the Juchitán PRI.

Interviewing the more savvy *priístas* was difficult because it was hard for me to restrain my disdain for the PRI. Most of the people I interviewed had to know or at least suspect that I was a COCEI supporter. Furthermore the *priísta* interviewees were in the difficult position of explaining to me why they as educated, modern people would support an obviously corrupt, authoritarian party. Usually the progressive *priístas* I interviewed chose to attack COCEI rather than defend their own party. Thus, I was told that COCEI was also corrupt or just as corrupt as the PRI, that COCEI had been a positive movement at the beginning but had gone downhill since, and that COCEI's claim to defend Zapotec culture was just a ploy to attract votes. Given that I did not agree with the political ideas of the *priístas*, I sought to establish common ground in other ways such as our shared interest in Isthmus culture, mutual acquaintances, and so on.

In the case of Elí Bartolo (a centrist gay intellectual then identified with the PRI), I was able to gain access to him through his brother-in-law Geoff Hartney, an Australian emigré married to Eli's sister. Geoff and his close friend Peter Hisscock, an Englishman also married to a Juchiteca, had been travelling around the world when they met Isthmus women, married them, and settled down with their families in Juchitán. Geoff married into one of the oldest, most traditional Zapotec elite families, whereas Peter married a working-class girl from the poor barrio of Cheguigo. Both Geoff and Peter were staunch working-class guys, but by virtue of their Europeanness and more worldly backgrounds than the local peasants, were thrust into the unlikely role of foreign elites in Juchitán. Because they were native English speakers and longtime residents of Juchitán, Geoff and Peter unwillingly became tour guides and key informants for visiting scholars and journalists interested in Juchitán's colorful political scene. Geoff, because of his involvement in his in-law's well-known and centrally located clothing store, was constantly called upon by visitors to explain local goings-on.

This created certain ironies because most of the visiting gringo intellectuals were upper middle class in their countries yet, in Juchitán, sided politically with the COCEI peasant organization they barely knew. Geoff and Peter, on the other hand, had been involved in tense conflicts with COCEI because of *coceísta* attempts to extract taxes or worker indemnities from their businesses. They viewed COCEI as a corrupt, manipulative organization "like all Mexican political parties," and they saw visiting scholars as naïve idealists akin to the so-called "Sandalistas" who flocked to support the leftist Nicaraguan regime. Geoff and Peter were generous and helpful in spite of their reservations about my research. It was ironic that they had seen COCEI develop first-hand and knew more useful ethnographic information about the Isthmus than I could ever hope to acquire, yet most of it meant little to them. What I considered juicy data were for them just bits of everyday trivia.

Through Geoff and his in-laws, I learned about the cozy lives of the Zapotec upper class. From Elí I heard about the viewpoints and dilemmas of Isthmus gays. Elí was a difficult interview because he considered foreign researchers nuisances (because of his progressive university education), and found my pro-COCEI stance irritating. The one area in which we could communicate well was Isthmus gender relationships. We saw eye-to-eye on the lack of equality for Isthmus women, despite the myth of matriarchal Zapotecs, and the need to improve the rights and living conditions of Isthmus *muxe'*. Thus, despite some tensions and disagreements with *priísta* interviewees, I was able to obtain useful information from our conversations.

Julio Bustillo, owner of the stylish Bar Jardín, was another difficult nut to crack. The Bar Jardín was one of the few places where PRI and COCEI intellectuals and activists mingled freely. Other well-known Juchitán bars and cantinas were more clearly identified with one faction or the other. I spent many afternoons and evenings drinking in Julio's bar, as did most of the visiting intellectuals as well as members of the local intelligentsia. The decor and atmosphere of the Bar Jardín somewhat resembled that of an upscale San Francisco coffeehouse. There were beautiful flowering plants in huge clay pots, a large native Isthmus tree in the open patio, bright paintings by Zapotec artists on the walls, and Nueva Canción music on the stereo.

Julio, the son of the powerful *priísta* Mario Bustillo, had been educated in Mexico City and had spent considerable time in Spain. He saw himself as a stylish, cultured entrepreneur interested in combining native Zapotec customs with modern ideas from the outside world. He also considered himself and his bar a kind of neutral zone where political ideologies could be set aside and progressive ideas exchanged. Of course, *coceístas* thought Julio was just another rich *priísta*. In our formal discussions, Julio behaved shrewdly, just like his tight-lipped father. From him, though, I learned how politicized and divisive on a personal, everyday level life in Juchitán had become. I also learned that some of the younger, more liberal *priístas* had some good ideas, but that the inertia, authoritarian structure, and deeply rooted corrupt practices of the Isthmus PRI prevented needed innovations from flourishing.

My interviews with *priístas* were few because my primary interests were COCEI's political tactics and ethnic ideology. Early in my fieldwork I observed a COCEI highway blockade near Tehuantepec in protest of insufficient government support of peasant agriculturalists. This event—recorded in my fieldnotes of November 18, 1991—illustrates COCEI's in-your-face style:

When I arrived at the highway to observe the COCEI blockade it was about 3:00 P.M. Cars were backed up from the main blockade located near the Hotel Calli all the way past the Hotel Tehuantepec to the big curve that leads to the entrance to town. The sun was beating down and it was sweltering. I parked the car near an abandoned gas station and walked about half a kilometer to the first blockade. En route I passed numerous big trucks, buses, and miscellaneous vehicles, including several belonging to frustrated tourists. People were waiting in their cars or sitting on top or alongside them while others went to the nearby bar to wait out the blockade while drinking beer.

The largest COCEI blockade consisted of about forty Zapotec peasants who were standing obstinately in the middle of the road. They also used a large number of branches of spiny green mesquite to block the highway—these were placed perpendicular to the road and would have punctured the average tire that ran over them.

A constant stream of people walked by; they were mainly angry travelers who had arrived by bus and who were forced to get out of the buses and walk from where the barricades began to their destinations. A small number of COCEI women wearing bright red rebozos, hair ribbons, *huipiles*, and *faldas* also blocked another part of the road. There were a couple of traffic cops around, and a truckload of soldiers arrived as I left the area to walk to the next barricade. These soldiers apparently did nothing to hinder the blockage and soon disappeared from view.

The Agricultural Ministry building was locked up and the entry gate closed because of the protest. A number of workers, or possibly COCEI supporters, were sitting inside the gate. Several *coceístas* were resting inside a discarded Pemex water pipe along the road. The heat was intense but the *coceístas* did not seem to have any water with them that I could see. They talked and laughed, seemingly at ease under the circumstances.

At one point an exasperated 18-wheeler driver pulled out of the left lane (facing Juchitán) of parked vehicles and headed down the right lane at a rapid rate of speed directly toward the *coceístas* who were blocking the road—immediately men and women picked up large rocks and poised themselves to throw them at the truck. I and others scurried out of the way fearing the truck would run into them. Some protesters yelled at the truck driver and several rocks were thrown in front of the truck. About thirty-five or forty feet from the barricade the truck came to a screeching halt and several more rocks were hurled in his direction. The driver then got out of the truck nonchalantly amid jeers and insults and walked a short ways away. At that point the *coceístas* relaxed a bit and some put down their rocks; others hung on to theirs as they had before this incident, including many women. This blockade was obviously well-planned and executed and seemed to be the work of people with considerable experience in such actions.

COCEI political protests like these were commonplace during my fieldwork. Gradually, as I attended COCEI demonstrations, hung out in Juchitán bars and the Cultural Center, attended fiestas and parties, and walked around town, I began to expand my base of contacts and friends among COCEI cadres and rank-and-file *coceístas*. Bit by bit I began to put together the mosaic of ethnic ideas and culturally based practices that motivated and sustained the COCEI movement. I learned that *coceístas* were motivated by Marxist revolutionary ideology but also viewed their struggle as the millennarian fight of mistreated Zapotec Indians seeking control over farmland, higher wages, and local political self-determination.

COCEI demonstrations were a kind of orchestrated political theater, with elements of spontaneity and humor. In these rallies, the movement's leaders eloquently espoused their political philosophy and galvanized the ethnic and class solidarities of *coceísta* intellectuals, workers, peasants, and students. On March 20, 1988 I attended one of the largest and most exuberant demonstrations since the destruction of COCEI's People's Government. This gathering was part of the 1988 presidential and local elections that COCEI participated in while affiliated with the Mexican Socialist Party (PMS) and the Cardenista Front.

Obdulia and I arrived at the rally in front of the freshly painted COCEI Central Committee office at about 11:30 A.M. There was already a massive crowd that stretched almost an entire block. At least half of the crowd was women. Both men and women wore red COCEI colors in every imaginable way: *huipiles* of innumerable designs, earrings, shawls, skirts, bandannas (around neck, forehead, and hair), flowers in the hair, T-shirts, blouses, braids, hats, handkerchiefs, shoes, pants, jackets, and belts. The *coceístas* carried and waved little red flags (made out of sticks or reed poles) with COCEI insignia lettering. Others waved banners with political slogans. Women attached red flags or balloons to their hair, as in fiestas. Vendors hawked fruit beverages and snacks. One man had written Alejandro Cruz's (a COCEI martyr) name on his cap.

The atmosphere of the rally was festive and joyous. Regional music played over the scratchy loudspeaker, people swapped jokes in the Zapotec language, and firecrackers or bottle rockets shot off as COCEI contingents arrived from the Juchitán barrios, nearby towns, and labor unions. The names of each arriving group were announced over the loudspeaker located on a platform in front of the office by one of the minor COCEI leaders who served as emcee. As the new groups joined the crowd they were greeted with loud cheers and band music. Enthusiastic supporters, like barkers, periodically cried out "Long live the peoples of the Isthmus!" The announcers repeated the names of the contingents and praised the unity of the Isthmus towns within COCEI. As the crowd grew we became more tightly packed along the narrow street. Instead of making people nervous this only encouraged their jubilation. Red confetti, poured on people's heads to mark their attendance, increased the festive atmosphere.

COCEI had worked hard to organize this event. This planning did not detract from the relaxed, informal mood of the gathering. The arrival of each bunch of rank-and-file *coceístas* was sufficiently synchronized that one group showed up right after the other, which caused the emotion and excitement of the audience to build and build. After all groups had arrived, the crowd proceeded to march through the populous fifth and seventh wards of Juchitán. Héctor Sánchez, a charismatic leader, walked around encouraging stragglers to join the march. Marchers chanted pro-COCEI phrases and yelled "Death to the PRI!" During this time, I joined the assemblage waiting at City Hall for the main part of the rally because it was my policy not to participate in COCEI marches for fear of deportation by the Mexican government.

At the plaza, a COCEI politician warmed up the audience with lively Zapotec music. Huge banners with COCEI and PMS insignia hung from the municipal buildings. The speaker's platform was the flat bed of a truck, long and wide enough to accommodate about thirty people. *El Machete* and *El Socialista*—the Socialist Party's buses—were parked to the south of the plaza. The place was crawling with photographers and journalists. Despite the fierce, uncomfortable winds and fiery sun, the turn-out for the event was somewhere between five and ten thousand people. Large numbers of the audience sat in chairs in front of the stage and others sat atop the little bookstore in the plaza or on top of trucks which brought people to the event. The whole area between the plaza and City Hall was full, and people were standing for another forty feet into the plaza's park.

The COCEI masses arrived at City Hall after a half-hour walk. The marchers were met with roars of applause. Heberto Castillo (the main PMS leader) walked arm-in-arm with Eraclio Zepeda (a noted leftist intellectual from Chiapas) and Daniel López Nelio of COCEI. Polín of COCEI acted as a moderator in a regal and dignified fashion. He introduced the visiting PMS dignitaries and the COCEI elite who stood on the platform. They all wore *guie' chaachi* and red gladiola wreathes around their necks. Daniel López Nelio, the COCEI peasant leader, had so many flowers draped around his neck that he looked comical, as he is very short and the wreathes stretched down to his knees. His diminutive, humble, if not comical, appearance contributed to his appeal to the masses as did his obvious mastery of Zapotec and his eloquence and force as a speaker.

After the introductions, the obligatory political speeches began. Zepeda gave a loud, dramatic talk which was well received. He praised

COCEI highly and used colorful metaphors about building socialism as if it were a large house where everyone would be welcome. Sánchez gave a short, but very powerful, talk in Zapotec in which he made fun of Mexican president Carlos Salinas de Gortari as *Gueu'tari*. *Gueu'* literally means coyote in Zapotec, but also has the double meaning of "*puto*" (faggot).

Polín gave a very clear and articulate talk in Zapotec and included a joke about how at the end of his term as deputy he would not pass on the *bastón de mando*, the staff of office, to López Nelio; "I will pass on the office but not the staff, because I will need that to walk with," he said. Finally, López Nelio gave his formal address. Although his beginning was somewhat slower, his emotion, energetic mannerisms (his favorite one being to point toward the sky with the index fingers of both hands pointed at a 45-degree angle bringing his hands up and back from his body forcefully), and sincerity stole the show. His talk was by far the most inspiring. López Nelio said that if the Agricultural Ministry did not give water to the peasants, he would personally take the COCEI crowd up to the Benito Juárez dam and open it himself so that the peasants could have water. He also said that if elected, his first act as a deputy would be to call for the presentation by the government of "Víctor Yodo," a COCEI activist disappeared by the military in the 1970s. Numerous times, the crowd chanted "¡Víctor Yodo Libertad!" (Free Víctor Yodo!).

López Nelio noted how Pemex has refused to pay San Blas peasants for damaging their fruit trees when it built a major oil pipeline.[2] He and Sánchez constantly pronounced the "o" of Spanish words as a "u" (e.g., "*Méxicu*") when speaking in Zapotec and they called the Isthmus towns by their original Zapotec names (e.g., *Guissi* for Tehuantepec). López Nelio's final remark was that of all the things he would do as an elected politician, "the most beautiful was to defend the Zapotec culture."

The atmosphere was lively and emotional with lots of jokes, impromptu cheers, chatting, and photograph taking. A call for contributions was well received at the end of the demonstration. At least 70 to 100 people gave money personally to the political leaders. Unfortunately, only two women politicians were on the stage, and no women addressed the crowd. Yet, there was obviously a strong leader—crowd identification and some dialogue took place between leaders on the platform and members of the crowd. The charisma of the Zapotec

speakers seemed to represent a stylistic element inherited from indigenous leaders of the past.

Although I began to understand the radiçal movement's impetus
through attendance at COCEI rallies and protests, I still had in the
back of my mind the desire to interview the three main COCEI leaders.
After sharing beers with Héctor Sánchez at fiestas, and chatting infor-
mally with him, I was finally able to arrange an interview with the
COCEI *jefe máximo*. Héctor invited Obdulia and me to his house for
dinner.

When I went to Héctor's house I found that it was located in a modest neighborhood (*la segunda sección*), but that it was clearly the best
house in the area. It was a modern, middle-class, Mexico City-style
dwelling with little that was distinctively Zapotec. Héctor's wife Lilí
was originally from a prominent (non-Indian) Mexico City family but
now dons the *huipil* and *falda* of Zapotec women. She has also played a
major role in organizing COCEI women. Despite Héctor's bona fide
reputation for drinking, womanizing, and brawling, the scene at dinner was strictly nouveau riche with proper upper-middle-class behavior
and etiquette. Héctor deftly avoided or ignored my probing questions
about COCEI history, organization, and ideology. Interviewing the
top COCEI politician was a wash-out. Fortunately, Lilí saved the day.
When the conversation faded or Héctor went off to talk to a bodyguard
or receive a phone call, Lilí entertained us with stories about COCEI
women's activities, the family lives of COCEI members, and other useful information about COCEI's internal functioning—in other words,
most of what I wanted to get from Héctor.

This experience reinforced my concerns about structured interviews. They simply were not well suited for discussing such a delicate
topic as radical politics, especially with people who had been jailed, tortured, and involved in numerous violent conflicts with their opponents. From the meeting with Héctor Sánchez I also learned the value
of establishing personal and family ties with my informants, rather than
hitting them up cold for an interview prior to any personal interaction.
The personal strategy eventually helped me gain access to Polín, the
most charismatic COCEI leader and the mayor during the movement's
heyday. Through my COCEI activist connections and experiences in
the Juchitán cantinas I made contact and developed a strong friendship
with "*Ta* Polo," Leopoldo de Gyves Pineda, Polín's father. *Ta* Polo is a
legendary figure in Juchitán because of his military exploits, political
activism, and role in the founding of COCEI.

In his seventies, *Ta* Polo was still a striking figure. Typically, when I saw him at the cantinas, at the COCEI demonstrations, or around town, he was dressed in a tight, dark brown suit, with a Texas-style brown felt cowboy hat, a red COCEI bandanna around his neck, and a copy of the day's newpaper sticking out of his back pocket. Polo exhibited a powerful masculine presence in the cantinas, where he was admired by the Zapotec peasants who frequented them. As we sat discussing Isthmus culture and history, grizzled old farmers would come up and shake *Ta* Polo's hand and refer to him respectfully as "Major," his former rank in the Mexican military. Because of his many years of activism in COCEI, during which he was imprisoned by the Mexican government and named a prisoner of conscience by Amnesty International, Polo was cautious with scholars and journalists. At one point, he told me that he knew I was trying to infiltrate COCEI and that he would not tell me anything secret.

Given this circumstance, and my decision to take the research slowly, my conversations with *Ta* Polo focussed on earlier periods in Isthmus history, such as the 1930s and 1940s, prior to the advent of COCEI. I learned from *Ta* Polo about the Isthmus past and eventually saw him so frequently that we became good friends. He finally let his guard down with me. Being seen so often with Polín's father (the grand old man of COCEI) undoubtedly played a role in being able to interview the son at his home. As with Héctor Sánchez, the interview took place during a meal accompanied by a few beers. Polín's house and manner were more relaxed than Héctor's and the conversation flowed more freely. Like Héctor, Polín emphasized COCEI's official ideology: that the movement was an ethnic one based on Zapotec cultural principles. But, unlike Héctor, he provided me with examples and anecdotes to illustrate his points. For example, he said that everything the *coceístas* did was rooted in Zapotec tradition, even mundane things such as drinking coffee, which is drunk out of a bowl with two hands the same way the ancient Indians drank from clay pots.

It was a thrill to finally interview the gifted young COCEI icon in his home. This legitimated my presence even more in Juchitán and provided me with valuable ethnographic data. Yet what was most revealing from the interviews with Héctor and Polín was not the overt content of what they told me but the style in which they presented their ideas and the details I could glean about their personalities and lifestyles. Having interviewed Polín and Héctor, the only remaining member of the triumvirate that I had not spoken with was Daniel López Nelio

("Nelio"), COCEI's fiery, folkloric peasant leader. My key informant in the Zapotec cultural movement, Macario Matus, said that Héctor and Polín were aristocratic leaders who cautiously protected their images, but Nelio liked to hang out in bars among the people. "*Nelio es el pueblo*" ("Nelio is the people"), Macario told me. In many ways Macario was right, and my discussions with Nelio were the most fruitful political interviews of my research.

I had seen Nelio several times in bars and spoken to him briefly before we finally connected for a long conversation over cold bottles of beer. Although Nelio was the most radical and volatile of the COCEI leaders, he was not physically imposing. Five feet tall at most and slightly built, Nelio often wore old, worn-out huaraches, frayed shirts, and the characteristic COCEI red bandanna around his neck. Until he became a federal deputy and had the resources to afford dental repairs, Nelio had a big gap in his smile where numerous teeth had fallen out. His hair is now grey, but in his younger years he sported a tousled mop of brown hair and at times a walrus-like, droopy moustache. If one did not know him, one might think that he was a poor peasant farmer. What Nelio lacked in physical presence, however, he made up for in charisma and personal power. When I hung out with him, older Zapotec men would constantly approach him to pay their respects.

Like the famous indigenous general Heliodoro Charis, Nelio is a man of the people whose strongest language is Zapotec. His Spanish is inflected with Zapotec accents. Also similar to Charis, Nelio has a wicked, picaresque sense of humor that he used to full advantage in COCEI political speeches and barroom klatches. Juchiteco allies often referred to him affectionately as a *lépero*, a sort of comical bad boy. Sometimes Nelio's humor was the inadvertent result of slip-ups in the Spanish language, just like Charis. One of the most developed genres of Zapotec folklore today are Charis jokes and verbal faux-pas, often invented and posthumously attributed to the famous Zapotec general. A typical Charis *cuento*[3] I collected during my interviews with the *coceístas* goes as follows:

General Charis had become an important general in Mexico City. One night he was attending a formal dinner for the top Mexican generals and their wives. General (and ex-president) Lázaro Cárdenas and General (and President) Manuel Avila Camacho were in attendance. As the evening progressed, each of the generals was asked to speak about the famous battles they had fought. When it was Charis' turn he said, in his faulty Spanish, that the greatest moments in his life were "*cuando me vengo*" (which can either mean "when I take revenge" or "when I come") because "*la venganza es lo más bonito en la vida, por eso me gusta venirme mucho*" ("revenge [or coming] is the most beautiful thing in life, that is why I like to come a lot"). The crowd listened in horror.

Although Nelio carried on Charis's rustic peasant accommodation to Spanish and the mores of Mexican national culture, he was also more well educated than he appeared. Nelio has a degree in sociology (like many of the *coceístas*) and has published several articles in academic and journalistic publications. Throughout our conversations, as his green eyes flashed wildly, Nelio made sophisticated literary and political references, which were also interspersed with double entendres in the Zapotec language and raucous laughter. Once, as I grabbed for a piece of sliced cucumber that we were eating with numerous *caguamas* of beer, Nelio said that he did not trust me because I was a capitalist who monopolized his beer and food.

Frequently when I went drinking the bartender would inform me that Nelio had been there the previous afternoon. When I met Nelio in the street he would playfully ask me "*¿Hay o no hay?*" ("Is there any or isn't there?"), referring to whether any beer was available or not. Stories and legends of Nelio's carousing and political tactics circulated freely among my Juchiteco friends. In our discussions, Nelio summarized his personal philosophy in terms of his four main pursuits in life: (1) women, (2) books, (3) drinking, and (4) politics.

Nelio revelled in his bad boy image. He described the Juchitecos to me as barbaric ruffians and, he continued, "I am their leader." He said that he would leave no wealth and inheritance, only a politically organized community. Nelio recounted his life to me and used it as a parable to explain why Juchitán is such a radical Indian community. He said that as a child he was taught to stare down rattlesnakes and wrestle (in a game known as *porrazo*) and fight with neighbor kids. His parents told him to beat the other kid or return home without crying. They taught him to be a man.

When Nelio returned to Juchitán, after his sociology training at the national university, he came with the intention of forming "red communes." He even named his first son "Lenin." Nelio said that COCEI was the result of the natural political evolution of Zapotec culture because the Juchitecos have always struggled for self-determination and their society is based on reciprocity and communalism from the family on up to the rest of the community. He said the Juchitecos fought through COCEI to preserve their language because "jokes are more humorous in Zapotec"; and "the Zapotec culture is the most beautiful thing on earth."

With Nelio I felt that I had finally gotten the real thing: unvarnished COCEI ethnic ideology from one of its architects and foremost practitioners. Nelio left posturing and secrecy aside and got right down to business. He was a superbly clear and intelligent informant who gave me exactly what I wanted. With the Nelio interview under my belt, I could finally relax and fill in the rest of the gaps in my fieldnotes at a comfortable pace without the anxiety I had previously felt.

As my interviews and discussions with *coceístas* deepened, I felt I had a good basic understanding of the movement. The movement was started in the early 1970s by a group of young university-educated Zapotec radicals. These young people—led by Nelio, Héctor, and Polín—had been inspired by the Mexican student movement of 1968, the growing critiques of the PRI's one-party rule, and the limited democratic openings of the Echeverría administration. They favored direct action tactics such as labor strikes, building takeovers, highway blockades, commandeering buses, hunger strikes, and marches. Their immediate goals were to obtain benefits for the Isthmus working class, peasantry, and students and to wrest political control of Juchitán from the corrupt local branch of the PRI. COCEI's structure consisted of about a dozen section committees in each of Juchitán's neighborhoods, a middle-level cadre of activists, the approximately sixteen-member directorate, and the three main leaders.

After successful strikes and protests in the 1970s that granted rights and concessions for students, peasants, and townspeople who used the local medical clinic, COCEI began to gain a large following among the poor and intellectuals of Juchitán. Several massacres of *coceístas* by police and government soldiers attracted more sympathy and support for the movement. A big part of COCEI's success can also be attributed to the talent and charisma of its leaders. Eventually COCEI, in alliance with the Mexican Communist Party, won the 1981 Juchitán municipal elections. This victory was possible because of COCEI's strong local following, the weakness and bungling of the local PRI, and the López Portillo admininstration's desire to project a democratic image at home and abroad. Juchitán became the first city in Mexico with a radical opposition government and it attracted the attention of world media.

The high point in the movement's history was COCEI's self-styled People's Government (the *Ayuntamiento Popular*) that controlled

Juchitán from 1981 to 1983. The COCEI administration was able to make changes to improve the lives of the working people of Juchitán despite boycotting by state government officials and harassment by local *priístas*. The movement was also effective at galvanizing Zapotec ethnic sentiments through the use of the Zapotec language in local government offices and demonstrations, the creation of a discourse that linked the COCEI struggle to the Zapotecs' historical fight for self-determination, and the promotion of Zapotec cultural projects, symbols, and events. Likewise Juchiteco artists celebrated the COCEI in their paintings, writings, and songs. A growing Zapotec cultural revival was ignited and inspired by the COCEI–PRI conflict. This movement flourished with the financial and moral backing of Francisco Toledo, a world-famous artist from Juchitán who supported COCEI. From 1981 to 1983 COCEI's People's Government became a kind of mecca of Mexican radicalism and a hotbed for avant-garde Zapotec cultural promotion and innovations.

In 1983, the *Ayuntamiento Popular* was thrown out of office by the Mexican military after a series of violent conflicts and a five-month occupation of Juchitán City Hall by COCEI militants. Several *coceístas* were murdered. Nearly 100 were jailed, 4 of whom were named prisoners of conscience by Amnesty International. The resultant global publicity made COCEI a cause célèbre for leftist activists and intellectuals in Europe and the United States. COCEI leaders became the darlings of the left in Mexico City and hordes of journalists, scholars, activists, and hangers-on descended on Juchitán in a miniature version of the international attention and media coverage that the Zapatista movement (EZLN) would attract to Chiapas in the 1990s. COCEI, like the EZLN, was viewed as a heroic movement of downtrodden Indians that was violently repressed by the corrupt, authoritarian Mexican regime.

Like so many other outside intellectuals, I was attracted to COCEI by social realist posters depicting proud, powerful Zapotec women valiantly resisting an oppressive system. I was inspired by the Zapotec cultural magazine (*Guchachi' Reza*) that celebrated the revitalization of Isthmus culture and the political struggles of COCEI and its precursors through sophisticated artwork, poems, and essays. I was also moved by the newspaper and *Proceso* accounts of how the Mexican government had killed and tortured *coceísta* activists. My passion for COCEI was heightened by my marriage to a Zapotec woman and my experiences in the Isthmus. Finally, my training by Marxist/feminist professors at the University of Wisconsin prepared me to support a radical Indian movement in southern Mexico.

My growing involvement and friendships with COCEI activists and artists increased my attachment to the movement. My attendance at the jubilant COCEI demonstrations, hanging out in bohemian Zapotec bars, dancing at the bacchanalian *velas*, and interactions with the Juchiteco intellectuals at the cultural center increased my romantic, personal feelings about COCEI. The movement had everything: it was politically progressive, culturally sophisticated, smart, stylish, and sexy.

In retrospect, and frequently during my fieldwork, however, I wondered exactly what my relationship (political, moral, personal, academic) to COCEI was, or should be. Did COCEI, in some sense, need me? Did I contribute to the movement or help them in any significant way? At the beginning of my fieldwork I would sometimes feel like a clown standing to one side of the COCEI demonstrations listening to the speakers attack the oppressive Mexican government and the capitalist exploiters from the United States. I stood out like a sore thumb: a gangly gringo dressed in a yellow *guayabera* and wearing my orange huaraches, my briefcase and field notebook held close to my side. What was I doing there? Was I just another groupie, another "Sandalista" attracted to colorful images of Indian radicalism? Wasn't I really just there because the movement was cool, the beer was tasty, and the living was good? Or was it simply a question of academic career advancement—choose a hot thesis topic such as a "new social movement" like COCEI and publish books and articles about it?

There has been much anthropological angst devoted to these topics. I do not claim to have the answer to the political and moral dilemmas created by cross-cultural fieldwork. I am familiar with the critiques of anthropology as a kind of intellectual imperialism or Orientalism, the handmaiden of colonialism, a form of power/knowledge that exploits our informants, a narcissistic Western pursuit. Mexican friends told me they considered North American leftists who study or hang around Mexican political movements parasites. I have read the critiques of U.S. scholars by the Zapotec intellectual Víctor de la Cruz and the scathing attacks on Western scholarship by Maya cultural activists (Warren 1998).

I do not claim to be immune to or above such criticism. I exhibited many of the flaws identified by such critiques. However, I think my research on COCEI was legitimate. One strictly personal reason is my marriage to a Zapotec woman and being the father of a Zapotec child. I also have many close friends from the Isthmus. I consider these part of a lifelong connection. On the political front, I feel that my published research helps legitimize and give publicity to COCEI and the Zapotec cultural movement.

Does this justify my research in the Isthmus? Did I "do the right thing"? On balance, did I give back more than I took? In answer to these questions I can only reply, *¿Quién sabe?* (Who knows?). I know that I established deep friendships and that aspects of my fieldwork were fun and adventurous. I know that my resulting publications gave me a tenure-track job and a modest reputation as an anthropologist. I hope that as many or more benefits accrued to the people I studied.

Perhaps the highpoint of my dealings with COCEI leaders was my interaction with Oscar Cruz López, then director of public works in the Juchitán municipal government, and later mayor. Oscar was a powerfully built, athletic, ebullient man. His eyes were coal black, his kinky hair tightly cropped, his thick goatee well trimmed. Oscar overflowed with vigor, enthusiasm, and good humor. He was well liked by men and women; he was a popular COCEI leader. Even *priístas* considered him acceptable. When Oscar entered a room, his positive attitude and sincerity were infectious. Unlike most of the politicians I encountered in my research, Oscar inspired trust. When he met you Oscar was quick to proffer a firm handshake or a thumping *abrazo*.[4]

Oscar's warmth and openness hid his toughness and years of experience in violent political struggles. As I got to know Oscar he told me about his early days as a student activist in junior high school. He recounted a COCEI student march through the streets of Tehuantepec that culminated in a rock-throwing brawl with local conservatives and police. Oscar described a later incident in which he, sporting a nine-millimeter Beretta pistol, and other COCEI militants took back the San Miguel Chimalapas City Hall from *priístas* who had prevented the legally elected government from taking office. This event is commemorated in a beautiful poem ("A Birth in the Mountains") by the assasinated Zapotec poet Alejandro Cruz, who was a participant (Campbell et al. 1993, 205). Oscar shared with me his experiences in numerous bloody altercations with *priístas* and soldiers, and how he hid out in a friend's house—sleeping under the rose bushes and other flowering plants that she grew to sell in the Juchitán market—during the period in 1984 when Mexican soldiers patrolled the Juchitán streets and systematically repressed COCEI activities. He narrated the legendary 1981 COCEI takeover of the Guatemalan embassy in Mex-

ico City to protest government repression of the movement. Oscar re-
called how he was beaten by a high-ranking Mexican political official
after being captured in the embassy. He was then jailed for six months
in military and civilian prisons.

After Oscar and I became friends and drinking buddies, he gave me
books and pamphlets, and helped me arrange contacts with COCEI
leaders and intellectuals. We drank his beer and he let me stay overnight
at his house. We danced at fiestas, drank at bars, and one memorable
night sang Isthmus songs with his guitar-playing friend Feliciano
Marín (also a COCEI cadre), recited poems, and carried on until I fell
asleep in a chair at Oscar's small house. Unlike the more arrogant
COCEI triumvirate, Oscar was accessible and sincere. His family background was modest; and although he was a rising star in the movement, he retained an innocence and generosity. With Oscar I felt I had
achieved something. He was not only a great informant, but also a true
friend. His daring exploits and dedication inspired me and heightened
my passion for the research and the COCEI cause. In many ways, Oscar
represented the best of what COCEI was about. Tragically, he was shot
and nearly killed by *priísta* gunmen during a political conflict in a small
Oaxacan town in spring 1999. At the time of this writing Oscar appears
to be recovering from his wounds. His example clearly illustrates the
risks and dangers of radical politics in rural Mexico, as well as the most
idealistic side of the COCEI movement.

NOTES

1. *Na* is the Zapotec diminutive for the Spanish *Señora*.

2. In a mixture of Spanish and Zapotec, López Nelio said that Pemex offers the peasants 45,000 pesos per tree, but each tree represents a million sac-
rifices by the peasant (*"ti yaga, Pemex ofrece 45,000 pesos; peru ti yaga ti
millión de sacrificios"*).

3. *Cuento* in Spanish means short story or tale. In the case of the Charis
cuentos, however, the best translation is probably "joke" because the Charis
cuentos are almost always humorous.

4. A form of ceremonial hug commonly exchanged by politicians, relatives, and business associates in Mexico.

CHAPTER 5

Zapotec Cultural Movement

The recent Isthmus Zapotec cultural revival movement began in Juchitán around 1972 with the founding of the Juchitán *Casa de la Cultura* (Cultural Center) by Francisco Toledo. Other important dates in the genesis of the movement were the founding of the cultural magazine *Guchachi' Reza* (Sliced Iguana) by Víctor de la Cruz in 1975, and the arrival of Macario Matus as cultural center director in 1978. Another major influence on the Juchiteco cultural revivalism was the COCEI political struggle that its leaders framed explicitly in ethnic terms.

Macario Matus, who skillfully managed the Juchitán Cultural Center until 1988, was my main informant about the Zapotec cultural movement. Under Matus's guidance, the center became one of the most important intellectual institutions in southern Mexico. The center is housed in former military barracks that occupy nearly one square block. Its large dark wooden doors, white-washed walls, high-pitched tile roof, and beautiful flowering trees in the courtyard provide a kind of cultural oasis from Juchitán's dusty, noisy streets. The narrow entrance to the building is typically plastered with 50–100 posters announcing previous or upcoming center events or artistic and cultural happenings in other parts of Mexico. At the time of my fieldwork, the walls of the entrance were also covered with a brightly colored space-age mural by a Mexico City artist named Tlatilpas.

Past the tunnel-like entrance, the center opens up into a rectangular open patio. There is also a bandstand with a mural by a Japanese painter at its base on the side facing the entrance.[1] In the background rises the tall yellow tower of San Vicente church. There are potted plants in large clay vessels along the walkways under the roof's overhang. The floor is made of worn red tile and there is a large garden in the left central portion of the patio. There is a stall in the entrance that sells books, magazines, tapes, and records by Zapotec people or about the Isthmus. A blackboard with announcements of upcoming events faces the entrance way. There is a wood sculpture by Víctor Orozco in one hallway. Posters displaying reproductions of old newspaper articles about the rebel leader Che Gómez and Juchitán during the revolution decorate the walls.

Surrounding the patio in small old-style rooms with high ceilings are archaeology and modern art galleries. During my fieldwork, one of the art galleries had an exhibit of original paintings by famous Mexican artists including Tamayo, Toledo, Zúñiga, Carrington, Cuevas, Nichisawa, Vlady, Belkin, Felguérez, Rojo, Siqueiros, Orozco, and others. Works by Isthmus artists Alfredo Cardona Chacón and Delfino Marcial were also on display. Adjacent to this gallery is a library and a current art gallery. Another room is for children and it contains chessboards, toys, taxidermized indigenous fauna from the region, and a reproduction of a primitivist painting by Miguel Covarrubias of a large-breasted Indian woman walking topless and carrying a basket on her head through an Isthmus village. Around the outer walls of the different rooms are rustic wooden benches—like church pews—known in the region as *bangu'*. The office of the director has a small library of books concerned with the Isthmus.

Because of its many activities and programs, the center was a mixture of an art museum, a culturally oriented YMCA, and a university student union. It was the artistic heart of the Isthmus, an important clearing house for intellectuals travelling through southern Mexico, and the springboard for myriad artistic creations, research projects, poetry conferences, and political meetings. Besides the large amount of cultural material (paintings, books, musical recordings, etc.) that the center provided me, it also helped me become part of the bohemian Zapotec intellectual scene that I found reminiscent of the U.S. Beat Generation. Like the Beat Generation, Zapotec painters, poets, and musicians are starving artists who rebel against mainstream social conventions, are politically opposed to the status quo, and are in search of new experiences through alcohol, marijuana, and sex. Unlike the U.S. Beats, Zapotec bohemians haunt cantinas rather than coffeehouses. They are firmly linked to an indigenous cultural tradition that they celebrate and reaffirm, rather than being dropouts from and opponents of their inherited culture (as was the case with the Beats).

The relaxed atmosphere of the cultural center, where many local people pleasantly spent the afternoon chatting, smoking cigarettes while lounging on the *bangu'*, or playing chess, was ideal for the glorifed conversations anthropologists call ethnographic interviews. I interviewed many Zapotec writers and painters at the center as well as at their favorite bars or funky art studios. At times we discussed the Juchiteco cultural/political movement during rowdy fiestas or during informal drinking bouts at their homes or mine in San Blas. In my fieldnotes (of January 4, 1993), I described a typical afternoon of research and hanging out with the Zapotec bohemians:

In the morning we [Obdulia and I] took a taxi to Tehuantepec, then a local bus to Juchitán. In Juchitán, we quickly grabbed a taxi to the *Casa de la Cultura*. Arriving at the *Casa* we saw Sabino López and delivered the paintings I was unable to sell from the Oaxaca exhibit in El Paso. He gave me a print in gratitude for selling some of his paintings. At the *Casa* I spoke to Delfino about an exhibit he wants to arrange in Tucson, El Paso, and Juchitán. He noted that he, Oscar Martínez, and others recently displayed their work in Puerto Rico. Oscar also said he had shown work in Costa Rica.

The *Casa* seemed to be thriving with its usual creative activities. We also spoke with Azteca de Gyves, who is studying art in Mexico City and was trying to contact Vicente Marcial about having a show of her work in Juchitán. Inside the *Casa* we talked with Heber Rasgado, who told us about his ten-day trip to Germany for performances in Berlin. Vicente Marcial also went with him. We spoke to Vicente, who was just back from a meeting at City Hall to try to get funds for the *Casa*'s activities from the new COCEI administration.

From the *Casa* we went to Los Tulipanes, a restaurant/bar where we listened to Florinda Guerra's son sing Zapotec folk songs accompanied by his guitar. Natalia Toledo recited one of her poems, and she and Delfino painted a mural of Zapotec and Aztec glyphs and images on the wall of the bar. Florinda, a singer and teacher, lives with Gregorio Guerrero ("Goyo"). Goyo is an artist from the state of Guerrero.

While the artists performed, we sat at a table and drank Coronas and ate *botanas* of shrimp fried in garlic, fried fish, *chicharrón* with avocado, and blood sausage. In our drinking and talking group were: on my left Obdulia; Marinella Miano, the Italian anthropologist; Florinda; Goyo; Delfino Marcial; Gustavo López (a painter and guitarist) and a brother of his; Carlos Manzo (a

Zapotec historian), his brother, and brother's wife; Oscar Martínez; Sabino López; and Felipe Carrere (a painter) on my right.

After a while, Oscar Cruz, now COCEI mayor, showed up with Guadalupe Ríos, a leftist journalist. Earlier we had gone to say hello to him at City Hall in his office, where he was surrounded by dozens of Juchiteco townspeople wanting favors and jobs. It was a moment of pride for both of us to shake hands and give the *abrazo* in City Hall with him now *presidente*.

At one point I left the bar with Carrere and Goyo and we smoked a "Flavio" [marijuana joint] at Goyo's house. We talked some to Marinella. She is finishing her M.A. at the UNAM on Juchitán regional identity and Mexican national identity. For a short time we were joined by Jesús Urbieta, a talented Juchiteco painter who resides in Mexico City, copies Francisco Toledo, and is now a serious alcoholic who suffers delirium tremens even though he is relatively young (perhaps 37), and has been successful—recently winning a prize (1990) for being one of the best young painters in Mexico.

The atmosphere at Los Tulipanes was a classic bohemian scene: jokes in Zapotec; music; *botanas;* poetry; intellectual conversation; decadent boozing and dope-smoking with a large group of unconventional painters, poets, intellectuals, and hangers-on of various sorts including "El Diablo," the obnoxious drunk who always begs money from me, gets thoroughly drunk, and insults people.

Another important Juchiteco intellectual salon was Natalia Toledo's apartment in Mexico City. Natalia, a poet and daughter of the famed painter Francisco Toledo, turned her funky apartment into a cantina on the weekends to raise money and create a lively artistic scene. The place was like a 1930s Greenwich Village speakeasy with illegal sales of beer and mescal, and spicy Isthmus-style *botanas*. On any given night there were famous Mexico City artists in attendance, along with visiting European intellectuals and, of course, whichever Juchiteco artists happened to be in the city at the moment.

My key informant, Macario Matus, deserves a separate chapter of his own. I have many fond memories of our conversations at the cultural center and at various bars and cantinas. The Macario Matus I remember was a roly-poly, short man dressed in cheap huaraches and old, worn slacks with a string for a belt. He sported a Cheshire Cat grin behind tilted bifocals. After he wrote a few poems or essays in the morning, Macario would take care of the center's business in a leisurely way, while engaging in brilliant repartee in Zapotec and Spanish with various painters, writers, and friends. After an obligatory game of chess or two we would wander off to a cantina, seldom earlier than noon and never later than 1:00 P.M. In the cantina, the jokes and code-switching

Zapotec/Spanish puns[2] would continue and get more sexual in character. We used to say that Macario was a genius for the first two hours as he slugged down slurps of his "whiskey" (actually cheap mescal drunk from a tall water glass). When those two hours passed, the trajectory was downward. As his speech slurred and his appearance became more disheveled, the sexual jokes were transformed into insults and *leperadas*,[3] the come-ons to women and men became more outrageous, the homosexual camping more exaggerated.

The latter part of his performance was one of the most interesting and amusing aspects of his humorous repertoire, albeit threatening to the more homophobic members of his intellectual entourage. One of his favorite lines was "I love to fornicate . . . even with women!" ("*¡Fornico mucho . . . hasta con mujeres!*") Another of his gems of wisdom was his observation that so-and-so (various conservative politicians or other rivals) were assholes and the only difference between him and them was that, although he was also an asshole, at least he knew he was one, but the others didn't even know they were assholes.[4] Macario also liked to tell outrageous stories or lies that are part of a Zapotec genre of oral lore known as *guenda rusiguii*.

Throughout Macario's irreverent routines one could pick up invaluable information about local history and folklore (some of which he has published in elaborated form in his *eroto-manías* column in *Unomásuno*), juicy political gossip, and detailed knowledge about local families and traditions. All of this was interspersed with learned comments about Mexican art and world literature and quotes from songs or poems by Yevtushenko, Roque Dalton, and López Velarde. Those of us in the audience paid for this wisdom by covering Macario's bar bill. Seldom did he contribute more than a token amount to the communal kitty and, on one occasion, he left me holding the bag for a huge bill that he had offered to pay at the Bar Jardín, but that I, having picked up a few tricks in the Isthmus, conveniently shirked by claiming that Macario was responsible, although I knew he would never pay.

In addition to the many things he taught me, Macario Matus showed me that the Zapotec linguistic/intellectual tradition was alive and vibrant, constantly recreating itself in conversation and action as well as in literary publications and artistic creations. His fluency in Zapotec and Spanish, as well as a kind of hybrid Zapotec/Spanish similar to Border Spanglish, and his deep knowledge of Zapotec culture, alongside an erudite appreciation of Latin American art and European literature, produced a cultural style that was both provincial and cosmopolitan. His commitment to art in the face of political repression was admirable. His outrageous hedonism was shocking and offensive to some, but I found it hilarious and exhilarating.

In the salon atmosphere of the Zapotec cantinas, I felt a camaraderie I have seldom experienced among U.S. intellectuals. The Juchitán intellectual milieu, whatever its flaws may have been, was less alienated than the U.S. academic scene I am accustomed to (epitomized by the American Anthropological Association meetings, known not so affectionately as "the meat market"). Verbal interaction among artists, writers, musicians, and political activists was constant and face-to-face, unmediated by e-mail, phone calls, and faxes. Moreover, the political ideas and actions of the Zapotec intellectuals really mattered; they had tangible consequences in the local COCEI versus PRI political conflict, unlike so much of the ivory tower hot air or cyber-communication produced by narcissistic, so-called postmodern intellectuals at North American universities.

I also learned from the bohemian cantina experience about the conditions that informed the painting and literature of the Zapotec intellectuals. The painters often produced in a semi-drugged, drunk, or hallucinogenic state; and this is reflected in some of the images in their work. In addition to making references to Zapotec folk traditions and symbols and the work of the great Oaxacan painters such as Toledo and Tamayo, the largely self-taught Juchiteco painters seek and attain altered states of consciousness through drugs, alcohol, and sex and use these states as inspiration and to achieve a creative space in which they operate. For example, the swirling skirts and riotously colored geometric *huipiles* of Zapotec women dancing at fiestas—perhaps as viewed from the standpoint of an exuberantly inebriated fiesta participant—appear in the paintings of Israel Vicente. Just as COCEI politics was fueled by passion—outrage at injustice and ethnic pride—the Zapotec art scene was inspired by the ecstatic emotions of the fiesta and cantina world.

The sexual intrigues men cultivate or discuss in cantinas and elsewhere also were an element of the intellectual scene I learned about from the Juchiteco bohemians. Macario Matus has written several books of sexual stories and inventions, including *La Noche de Tus Muslos* (*The Night of Your Thighs*), *Poerótica*, and translations to Zapotec of erotic tales from *1001 Arabian Nights.* Francisco Toledo's paintings of sexual couplings between humans and animals and between animal species such as crabs, turtles, and fish reflect Zapotec mythology about the transformation and metamorphosis of selves and the pagan naturalism of peasant Oaxaca. Esteban Rios's "*Cinco Desmandamientos*" (*Five Mis-Commandments*)[5] displays the sexual obsessions and devotion to physical pleasure that are so much a part of life in the Isthmus, especially in Juchitán.

The Zapotec cult of women vividly illustrated in Alejandro Cruz's famous poem about "Lucía Zenteno";[6] Miguel Angel Toledo's paintings of sexualized Juchiteca matriarchs; Henestrosa's traditional song "Petrona"; "Naela," a song by Chuy Rasgado; and the Isthmus anthem "La Zandunga"; and thousands of paintings, songs, and poems about women by almost every Zapotec creative talent are other central components of Juchiteco intellectual production. In the cantina environment, I learned from Isthmus men about amorous adventures and troubles that were the raw materials that they recreated in their artistic and literary paeans to women. I also saw that the myth of Zapotec matriarchy or the anthropological claim of an Isthmus society of gender equality was bogus. Sex for the men I met in the cantinas—whether with their lovers, prostitutes, or *muxe'*—was a sport that they engaged in whenever possible to satisfy their desires. Drinking was an obligatory part and pleasure of male life. Both often occurred at the expense of marital and family relations as well as economic well-being. Zapotec women were celebrated and placed on carefully crafted ethnic pedestals in the creative output of the Zapotec intellectuals, but in daily practice they used women for their own satisfaction.

Through my cantina fieldwork, I also gained insight into the role of COCEI politics as an impetus and inspiration for Juchiteco art and literature. Isthmus painters like Oscar Martínez (nicknamed "*el araña*," the spider, because of his uncanny ability to scale walls and buildings in order to paint pro-COCEI political graffiti and murals) cut their teeth on political protest murals and banners, and exalted the movement and its symbols (red flag and white star, the COCEI insignia, etc.) in their paintings and prints. These artistic productions played a key role in local politics. At times during my fieldwork it seemed like almost every house or wall in Juchitán was covered with political propaganda, slogans, denunciations, murals, and campaign promises.

Many of the murals cleverly combined *coceísta* political messages with images of Isthmus animals, the tropical Isthmus landscape, or a Zapotec woman's *huipil* in the form of a COCEI banner—all depicted in shockingly bright colors. During the late 1970s and early 1980s, the mere act of painting leftist political graffiti could land one in jail. Much of the pro-COCEI artwork was temporary, known by the painters as ephemeral art because it was quickly whitewashed or destroyed by property owners or *priístas*. Sometimes the political art quoted verses from leftist revolutionary writers like Pablo Neruda, Roque Dalton, or the Zapotec writer Alejandro Cruz. Other times the street art contained stylized images of Che Guevara or Sandino. The cruder street painting consisted simply of slurs against rival politicians, such as the person's name followed by the words "faggot," "coward," or "corrupt," or the ever-popular "death to [the name of a *priísta*]."

Folk songs, *corridos*, and poems, were also key political weapons. For example, Israel Vicente paid homage to the COCEI political struggle in the Nueva Canción anthem dedicated to Lorenza Santiago, a pregnant woman who was murdered by members of the PRI and became a COCEI martyr. Alejandro Cruz wrote the stunning protest poem "*Hagamos una Pinta al Cielo*" ("Let's Paint a Political Protest on the Heavens!") in outrage at PRI/government violence, then ironically he was murdered by PRI bullets, and his poem became his own eulogy on the painted walls of Juchitán.

During my fieldwork, I began to collect and eventually amassed a large collection of protest literature, poetry chapbooks, grammars of the indigenous language, local histories, academic studies, and cultural magazines produced by Zapotec writers (most of whom supported COCEI). These ranged from poorly printed, precariously stapled pamphlets that soon fell apart and were mainly distributed among friends, to substantial books published by the best Mexican presses. The international attention Juchitán received as a result of COCEI's political success gave Isthmus Zapotec writers greater possibilities for publication than they had ever had in the past. Furthermore, the heroic and tragic events of COCEI history provided rich material for Zapotec authors. But the recent Isthmus writers also built on an earlier history of local literary production that is perhaps unique among indigenous groups in Mexico.

The first significant writings by Juchitán authors appeared in the 1930s in *Neza* (originally spelled *Nesha*), a publication of the New Juchiteco Student Association in Mexico City. Although this miniscule newsletter, which initially sold for five *centavos*, did not have much of an impact in the metropolitan world of Mexican letters, it was a major accomplishment for Indian people in a white- and mestizo-dominated country. The romantic idealism of *Neza*'s nativist ideology (which later informed the literary works of pro-COCEI intellectuals) is expressed in an exhortation by Gabriel López Chiñas to his fellow Istmeños on the front page of the first issue:

The new generation of Juchiteco students, feeling the strength of youth in its veins and in its spirit the need to guide the culture in our towns, has decided to organize a new Association and let go of all vile thoughts and bring to fruition the task that for many years the Isthmus region has cried out for. The new shoots bud, flourish, and bring fruit. (*Neza* 1987, 1)

López Chiñas's celebrated poem "The Zapotec Language" expresses the pivotal role of the native tongue in the Zapotec cultural movement:

> They say that Zapotec is going,
> no one will speak it now,
> it's dead they say, it's dying,
> the Zapotec language.
>
> The Zapotec language
> the devil will take it away,
> now the sophisticated Zapotecs
> speak Spanish only.
>
> Ah, Zapotec, Zapotec!
> those who put you down
> forget how much their mothers
> loved you with a passion!
>
> Ah, Zapotec, Zapotec!
> language that gives me life,
> I know you'll die away
> on the hour of the death of the sun.[7]

Neza's contents included articles about Oaxacan history, discussions of local customs, poems in the native language, notes on the spelling of Zapotec words, and statements of ethnic pride. Such writings are sometimes criticized as amateurish, antiquarian and provincial. There is a real danger of excessive quaintness and lack of quality in regionally focused literature. Yet, Juchiteco writing displayed an intensity and devotion to artistic creation, coupled with a political commitment to the survival of Zapotec culture in a rapidly industrializing society, that gave it social relevance and made it transcend the strictly local. The Zapotec writers, scraping together their pesos, produced works of lasting historical interest that also demonstrate the best aspects of the creative spirit. With little hope of commercial promotion, or international or national recognition, the Juchitecos developed a literary tradition of some merit that has continued to the present. While this may not be unusual in the wealthy countries of Europe and the United States, it was hardly common in the first half of the twentieth century among indigenous peoples from rural Mexico. *Neza*, and its successors *Neza Cubi* and *Guchachi' Reza*, were vital organs for the preservation of Isthmus Zapotec culture, and the emergence of a Zapotec intelligentsia that later bolstered COCEI.

Macario Matus, my main informant, founded *Neza Cubi* in 1968 during the highpoint of the radical Mexican student movement. In an epigraphic poem at the beginning of the first issue, Matus (*Neza Cubi* 1968, 2) heralded:

A new road[8]
a new path
a reopened road
that our ancestors walked
this is the purpose of *Neza Cubi*
New Road
. . .
In search of the footprints they left us
to reconstruct them
to be able to follow the path
and later walk, brothers,
fellow Zapotecs
toward the illuminated path of progress

Like its predecessor *Neza*, *Neza Cubi* showed off the poetic talents and cultivated knowledge of Zapotec linguistics of the Juchiteco intellectuals. In spite of the modernization rhetoric of Matus's poem, writers in *Neza Cubi*, reflecting the increasing radicalization of Zapotec students, denounced the impoverished living conditions of most Istmeños and the cruelty of the 1968 Tlatelolco massacre of students in Mexico City. Some of my main informants, including Matus and Víctor de la Cruz, participated in *Neza Cubi*. By the time I began my fieldwork, many of the Juchiteco intellectuals and activists were already seasoned veterans of radical politics in Mexico City and Oaxaca City, and hard-core bohemians. I received a profound political and cultural education in the hands of these colorful characters. As I mingled with and learned from the Isthmus writers and politicians, I fancied myself in the long tradition of other non-Zapotec intellectuals who had sojourned in Juchitán including

Miguel Covarrubias, Diego Rivera, Frida Kahlo, José Vasconcelos, Langston Hughes, Graciela Iturbide, and Elena Poniatowska.

The most recent Zapotec cultural journal, *Guchachi' Reza*, edited by Víctor de la Cruz, began to appear in the mid-1970s. Far more than previous Juchiteco publications, *Guchachi' Reza* possessed a cosmopolitan sophistication that compared with that of stylish Mexico City literary magazines. Each issue of *Guchachi' Reza* contained a full-color cover of high-quality photographs or avant-garde art by noted Mexican painters like José Luis Cuevas and Francisco Toledo. The inner pages were also embellished with reproductions of work by Vlady, Miguel Covarrubias, and others, and ethnographic or historical photographs of Zapotec life. The written material consisted of poems by Isthmus authors, archival documents, political manifestos, prose narratives, grammars of the Zapotec language, and other items by or about native people. The result was an eclectic and entertaining Zapotec studies journal.

Perhaps the most noteworthy piece of writing from the *Guchachi' Reza* generation of Isthmus intellectuals is the lyrical poem "Who Are We? What Is Our Name?" by Víctor de la Cruz, excerpts from which follow:

> Speech. Saying yes to the night,
> saying yes to darkness.
> Whom to speak with, what to say
> . . .
> Who got these words down on paper?
> Why write on paper at all
> instead of on the ground?
> Earth is huge,
> broad, extensive.
> Why don't we write below the sky's surface
> everything our minds speak out,
> everything born in our hearts?
> Why don't we write on the green leaves,
> on clouds, on water,
> on the palm of the hand?
> . . .
>
> Who brought that second language
> coming to kill us with our own word,
> coming to trample down our people
> as if we were maggots
> fallen from trees, scattered over the ground?
> Who are we? What is our name?[9]

In this poem, de la Cruz evokes the contemporary Zapotecs' struggle to understand their past and come to grips with their identity in a
bilingual (Spanish-Zapotec), postcolonial present. In another poem
("My Companions Have Died") that exemplifies the literary production by Juchiteco authors during the height of COCEI political conflicts with PRI, Macario Matus laments the killings of *coceístas* by
reactionary assailants:

> Mine—whom I never met
> but loved with all my soul.
> They seeded the fields
> but the day the land was taken
> that was the end of work.
> One time they were sent off to be outraged:
> On that day they climbed the sky's crags.
> And not only they have gone:
> together with our own went one
> who could read the word and was great.
> Over there where they murdered them,
> we were taught what life is,
> what a life of struggle has to be.
> They taught us the gist of liberty:
> that no one must trample on no one
> in this immemorial land.
> The day they quit, the sun died,
> the light left for another part of the day
> and no light remained to our solar kingdom.[10]

As the Matus poem illustrates, the most recent group of Juchiteco
writers, many of them my primary informants, connected their artistic
work with political activism. These topics were always in the air at the
COCEI-oriented cantinas—they filled our conversations and my field
notebooks. Our bohemian drinking circle was composed of an ever-
changing cast of characters who floated in and out of the *Casa de la
Cultura*. The core group consisted of Macario Matus; Juchiteco painters Sabino López, Miguel Angel Toledo, and Oscar Martínez; and musicians such as Heber Rasgado. We were frequently joined by other
Isthmus intellectuals and COCEI activists as well as journalists, poets,
painters, and social scientists from out of town who were studying
Juchitán. Although most of the visiting intellectuals were from Mexico
City, others were from Europe, the United States, and Japan. For a
small Indian city in southern Mexico, Juchitán had a remarkably fertile

and cosmopolitan intellectual and art scene. The result was a crossfertilization of ideas and projects that produced numerous books, poems, songs, and paintings.

The bohemian cantina/salon milieu was the main setting for my investigations of Zapotec creative activity. In this pleasant environment I learned about the main issues that propelled my anthropological research and also participated in a number of Isthmus-oriented cultural projects. These included a local oral history contest in which I won a prize; the Zapotec cultural magazine *Guchachi' Reza*, to which I contributed and later helped fund with book royalties; a local newspaper that published excerpts from my work; a multicolored mural of Isthmus animals painted on an inner wall of Obdulia's family's house; the book *Zapotec Struggles* (1993), and an issue of the *Rio Grande Review* that included writings and art of numerous Isthmus intellectuals. I also bought dozens of paintings from my starving artist friends.

Although my research with the local intelligentsia was largely successful, there were a few difficulties. One of these was interacting with the brilliant Zapotec writer Víctor de la Cruz, who, along with Macario (and Francisco Toledo from a distance) were the main pillars sustaining the recent Isthmus cultural revival, and are intellectual figures analogous to the Maya cultural activists studied by Warren (1998). Víctor had already written pointed criticism of another U.S. researcher in his magazine *Guchachi' Reza*. Even Víctor's close friends in COCEI and the Juchiteco cultural movement warned me that he was a sensitive person. Armed with this knowledge, I approached my first meeting with Víctor with caution. Fortunately, I was introduced to Víctor through my good friend Oscar Cruz. We spent the night drinking and carousing; but I refrained from asking pointed questions and just went with the conversational flow, emphasizing humor and lightheartedness in tune with the local style. Later, once he knew me, Víctor allowed me to question him about various topics at a small bar in the front room of a house near his family home.

There were at least three tense moments with Víctor. One was when he upbraided me for having juicy fellowships when he had little funding for his own research and writing, even though he had written at least a dozen books and numerous articles and poems. Another was when we were conversing in front of the COCEI office prior to a political demonstration and I overheard him warn a *coceísta* activist in the Zapotec language about the dangers of having a *dxu'* (outsider) in the house. The third incident involved his displeasure with an article I published in an Oaxacan academic journal (*Cuadernos del Sur*) about the Juchiteco intellectuals. These difficulties were overcome through boozing camaraderie (on one occasion we bonded because we were both hungover, after he said to me "*estás crudo?*"[11]) and through my ability to publish several pieces of his work in *Zapotec Struggles*, bring him to El Paso for a scholarly conference, and donate the royalties from *Zapotec Struggles* to a Zapotec cultural organization he cofounded. I knew our relationship had survived minor spats when he bought me drinks on one of my last visits to Oaxaca—a sure sign of amity in that setting.

As I got closer to the Zapotec artists and intellectuals, our interactions occurred more within the context of friendship and mutual self-interest, rather than in the more utilitarian anthropologist–informant relationship. Unlike the COCEI politicians, with whom I became friendly despite their initial suspicions but ultimately stayed at a distance from, with the artists, musicians, and writers I could open up and share my feelings and felt that they did the same. Many of the painters and writers eventually visited me in San Blas and some of them came to my house in El Paso, where I sold many of their paintings. I constantly helped the painters financially and frequently paid their bar bills. I spent many hours with them in their run-down studios, such as that of Miguel Angel Salinas, that I described in my fieldnotes as follows: "His workshop is an apartment with little furniture and bare cement floors. Recently-finished paintings hang from the walls and there are drips of paint on the floor, stacks of finished paintings in the corners of rooms, a table overflowing with tubes of paint, loaded ash trays, more paintings, photos of paintings, brushes, etc. On the floor are empty liquor bottles."

Hanging out in the artists' studios, homes, and the bars frequented by the Zapotec intellectuals, I was able to achieve the ethnographic depth I sought. With the COCEI politicians and activists I could obtain interviews, attend demonstrations, observe protests, and read political pamphlets and other literature. But there were clear obstacles to penetration of the movement. Meetings of the COCEI political directorate were clearly off-limits, and I thought it was a poor idea to attend the periodic neighborhood committee gatherings. Furthermore, I could never gain access to the back-room conversations and secret negotiations that were the lifeblood of Isthmus politics. Fortunately, my relationships with the artists and intellectuals allowed me to get behind the scenes and experience Zapotec cultural revival activities from the inside. I watched the painters paint and the sculptors sculpt, I listened to the poets recite their verses, and I sang along to the music of the Zapotec singer/songwriters.

I could verbally praise COCEI politics and write articles in support of the movement, but that was the limit of my efforts at solidarity. In the case of the writers and painters, I could publish their works. In El Paso I was able to create a museum exhibit of the Zapotec painters' works accompanied by traditional music played by Juchiteco musicians Heber Rasgado and Israel Vicente. I also helped several painters show and sell their works in El Paso when they came to visit. With the Zapotec artists and intellectuals I felt true collaboration was possible, transcending the colonial subject–object relationship that has plagued anthropology historically.

As with COCEI politics, I found that interviews with elite members of the Zapotec cultural movement—in this case Andrés Henestrosa and Francisco Toledo—were less satisfying than my ongoing contacts with the less well-known artists and intellectuals working in Juchitán. In line with Marcus's injunction to conduct "multisited" fieldwork (Marcus 1998), I interviewed Henestrosa in his office on Motolinía Street in Mexico City. The most famous living Oaxacan writer, Henestrosa (in his early nineties at the time of this writing), has also had a long career as a politician affiliated with the PRI. Despite his conservative politics and opposition to COCEI, Henestrosa's writing, especially his famous book of creatively embellished Zapotec myth and folklore *Los Hombres Que Dispersó la Danza*, is considered the foundation of modern Zapotec literature and an inspiration to Juchiteco cultural revivalists.

What was especially valuable about the Henestrosa interview was the way he illustrated and embodied the hybrid, constructed nature of recent Zapotec cultural production. Although Henestrosa claimed to be of humble Indian origin and still spoke Spanish with a distinctive Isthmus Zapotec accent, he had become a federal deputy, and later senator, in the Mexican legislature and an ally and confidant of Mexican presidents. My interview with him was interrupted by a phone call from Carlos Hank González, one of the richest and most powerful men in Mexico. This was interspersed with jokes and Isthmus anecdotes in the Zapotec language, primarily for Obdulia's benefit since my knowledge of Zapotec was then limited. Henestrosa was fully a part of Mexican national society but also a leading force in defining Zapotec culture (e.g., he was the director of *Neza*).

In response to my interview questions about historical changes in Zapotec culture, Henestrosa recounted rich memories of his interactions with famous Mexican intellectuals, politicians, and artists who had influenced or depicted the Isthmus in their work, including Diego Rivera and Miguel Covarrubias. Henestrosa boasted that he had provided Covarrubias with much of the information for his famous book *Mexico South*, in my opinion still the best book written about the Isthmus of Tehuantepec.

Although Henestrosa may have exaggerated his role in the making of the Covarrubias book, it was clear to me that he was illustrating the complex pathways of information flow between outsiders and local Zapotecs that are reproduced in canonical works, like *Mexico South*, that have become the best known representations of Isthmus Zapotec society. Just as Henestrosa had a hand in the Covarrubias book, his own book has come to be viewed as "typical" of the "essential" elements of Zapotec culture. He claimed that his book was based on legends and stories that were at least 200 years old, since they were told to him as a small boy by his nearly 100-year-old grandmother. Yet in the same breath he noted that his book also contained literary reworkings and recreations. The great Oaxacan writer also reinforced the notion of Zapotec cultural hybridity by describing how Zapotec Indians who come to Mexico City are changed, but become "neither [fully] Westernized nor cease to be Indians."

Although Henestrosa clarified important points about how what is known today as Zapotec culture is a product of earlier inventions, constructions, and hybridity, he could not resist invoking essentialist images of Juchiteco ethnic identity and pride that are key symbols and motifs of both the COCEI political movement and recent Zapotec cultural revival activity: "the Juchiteco has always been the same ever since he was born on earth . . . Juchitecos have always rebelled . . . Juchitecos are proud to speak Zapotec . . . they are all barbaric." These notions of an essential Juchiteco character that is tough, independent, and primal, and a Zapotec culture that is continuous and enduring are fundamental elements of Zapotec ethnic politics and cultural revitalization.

Interviewing Francisco Toledo, one of Latin America's best-known artists, turned out to be impossible. Notoriously shy, Toledo avoids and declines interviews by the dozen. In my case, I was able to have a brief conversation with him on the streets of Oaxaca City and through correspondence obtain two reproductions of his paintings for *Zapotec Struggles* (Campbell 1993) (one of which appeared on the cover).

When I encountered Toledo, he was dressed in his signature white cotton "Indian" pants and shirt and cheap huaraches. Obdulia spoke to him briefly in Zapotec and I also exhanged a few words with the famous painter. Toledo appeared meek, and spoke in a near-whisper. I quickly realized that Toledo preferred to let his brilliant Oaxacan art speak for itself rather than submit to ethnographic interviews.

Through my conversations and experiences, I also learned from the Zapotec intellectuals about their internal struggles and rivalries with fellow artists as well as the tensions between elements of the Zapotec cultural circle and the COCEI political movement that at times seemed to overlap. For example, Miguel Angel Salinas, a mestizo painter from Salina Cruz, Oaxaca, who does not speak Zapotec, told me repeatedly about what he called the racism of the Juchitecos. He said the Zapotecs from Juchitán discriminated against him for not being a Juchiteco although they also somewhat affectionately called him a *xhuncu* (literally "youngest son"; in this case it meant something like "shirttail relative") since he was from Salina Cruz. Miguel Angel also told me a humorous story about how the Juchiteco painters have a hard time adjusting to life in Mexico City when they go to promote their artworks, and quickly have to return to Juchitán. He cleverly mimicked the gestures of a provincial wood sculptor named Victor "Chaca" ("The Woodpecker") Orozco as he arrived in Mexico City and stared in awe and fear at all the cars, buildings, and people.

Miguel Angel's wife told me that most of the Juchiteco painters are repetitive, lazy, and poorly educated. She noted the general irresponsibility and drunkenness of Juchiteco men. She said the best and most creative of the young painters is Sabino López; the rest are much too regionalistic—their great defect. They know little about world art trends. Miguel Angel said that he was the only Isthmus painter of his generation who has left behind the regionalistic, Zapotec-oriented, Toledo-influenced painting mode. He has set off in new directions that are more surreal. His work is now more abstract, hallucinatory, and geometric, and includes images of European cities and churches. Miguel Angel also showed me some plans to create Leonardo da Vinci-influenced machines. These were comical machines, whimsical Rube Goldberg-like apparatuses with no real function. He planned to make them out of metal as sculptures.

According to Miguel Angel, the Isthmus painters are now divided and do not cooperate with each other, unlike the mid- to late-1980s when they were more united. Each painter looks out for his own interests. They will not tell each other about invitations to expositions and the like. He also criticized their lack of discipline, organization, and responsibility. Miguel Angel insisted that he has prospered by leaving the Isthmus—and the drunken, decadent atmosphere he criticized—and expanding his horizons and working and studying in Mexico City. He said the other Isthmus painters should do this, but they do not because of their provincialism. They refuse to leave Juchitán, where they have good food, women, beer, bars, a well-established social scene, nice weather, and Zapotec customs. They cannot adapt well to city life. He said they also do not know how to promote their work to galleries and art stores.

In addition to internal conflicts and personal weaknesses, the Isthmus intellectual scene was also hampered by political conflicts. One conflict was the fact that *coceísta* painters often had to sell their work to, or through, their political rivals in the PRI because most of the surplus wealth in the community was in the hands of *priísta* businessmen and politicians. This issue came to a head in the case of Julio Bustillos's Bar Jardín, one of the few places where *priístas* and *coceístas* comfortably mixed. Julio adorned his bar with paintings by local artists, most of whom were supportive of COCEI. Some of the artists, for ideological reasons, refused to show their works in the Bar Jardín; others harshly criticized Julio for charging a 30 percent commission for selling art to the bar's patrons. Still other artists, in a controversial move, chose to seek funding or patronage from the PRI mayor's office.

There were also conflicts between some of the Zapotec artists and the COCEI. For years, pro-COCEI Isthmus painters like Oscar Martínez and Sabino López painted wall murals, protest banners, and other political paraphernalia. COCEI leaders called this labor *tequio*, a traditional Oaxacan custom in which adult males donated several days of work each year to improve local roads and other municipal facilities. Eventually, some of the painters tired of donating "*tequio*" labor to the movement; they wanted to be paid. Yet other conflicts occurred between the COCEI leaders and Macario Matus, the cultural center director, whom the *coceísta* politicians sometimes viewed as not radical enough. Matus also feuded with the cultural center and artistic movement's main supporter, the wealthy artist Francisco Toledo. Additionally, Víctor de la Cruz, a leading Zapotec writer, came into conflict with the COCEI leadership.

For all of these reasons, the Juchiteco cultural scene was far from harmonious or trouble-free; yet there was something noble about the dedication of the Zapotec artists who worked for days painting colorful wall murals, only to have them wiped out by insipid PRI political propaganda during the next election. Other painters created beautiful images on the walls of sordid cantinas or sold charming paintings for the price of a pitcher of beer. Indeed, many of their creations were short-lived; some paintings fell apart rapidly because the artists could not afford top-quality materials. Much creativity and inspiration went into tiny chapbooks, limited circulation art magazines, and obscure lithograph print runs; but this never seemed to discourage the artists as long as they could buy the next beer or establish successful liaisons with women. Indeed, one of the most touching moments of my fieldwork occurred one day in the Juchitán Cultural Center when a poor, unsophisticated peasant guitar player came to Macario Matus to "register" (perhaps the man was thinking in terms of a copyright) a love song he had written in Zapotec so that it would not be copied by others. Macario told me the song was perhaps not of great artistic quality, but that there was a local tradition that one might call "grassroots songwriting" in the poor neighborhoods of Juchitán.

In my analysis, COCEI in the political arena, and the artists and intellectuals through their creations, were the two most powerful engines for defending and recreating the Isthmus Zapotec culture and identity in an era of profound economic, political, and ecological change. Both groups emphasized the preservation and strengthening of the Zapotec language, the valuing of Isthmus customs, the political struggle for self-determination, and the intense Juchiteco ethnic identity. To a small degree with COCEI, but especially in my interactions with the Zapotec artists and intellectuals, I felt that I could collaborate in ways that were supportive of their goals.

NOTES

1. Aspects of this description of the Juchitán Cultural Center have undoubtedly changed since my main period of fieldwork in 1987 and 1988.

2. A typical such pun would be for someone to call Oscar Cruz, a COCEI leader, "*mi amigu*," literally "my friend" with the "o" of "*amigo*" changed to a "u," as is common when Juchiteco speakers speak Spanish. "*Migu*" (or "*migo*") is the Isthmus Zapotec word for monkey, hence the person was also jokingly referring to Oscar as his monkey ("the monkey" is also Oscar's boyhood nickname).

3. *Leperadas* are amusing, vulgar comments.

4. As I recall, Macario would say it more or less like this "*Todos éstos que ves allí son unos pendejos y la única diferencia entre ellos y yo es que mientras yo también soy un pendejo, pero por los menos, sé que lo soy, pero en cambio ellos, ni siquiera, saben que son pendejos.*"

5. The Five Mis-Commandments are, essentially, the following:

    1. "thou shall love women"

    2. "thou shall adore beer"

    3. "thou shall fondle words"

    4. "thou shall mingle with prostitutes and homosexuals"

    5. "thou shall hate the bourgeoisie"

6. The poem is called "*La Mujer que Brillaba aún más que el Sol*" ("The Woman who Outshone the Sun") (Cruz Martínez 1991).

7. López Chiñas's original poem in Zapotec and Spanish can be found in *La Flor de la Palabra* (de la Cruz 1983, 68–69). The English translation is by Nathaniel Tarn and was published in *Zapotec Struggles* (Campbell et al., 1993, 211).

8. "New road" is the meaning of the Zapotec phrase *neza cubi*.

9. For the original poem in Zapotec and Spanish, see de la Cruz (1983, 81–83). The English translation by Tarn is in Campbell et al. (1993, 117–118).

10. See de la Cruz (1983, 76–77) for the original. The English translation by Tarn is in Campbell et al. (1993, 155).

11. "Are you hungover?"

CHAPTER 6

An End and a Beginning

The high point of my fieldwork was my birthday party in San Blas in May 1988, at which a mural of Isthmus animals and vegetation painted by Miguel Angel Salinas in Obdulia's family's home was displayed to Juchiteco visitors for the first time. Macario Matus and other members of the Juchiteco cultural movement attended, along with Oscar Cruz and various COCEI activists. At that point I realized that I had been accepted into the two main Zapotec milieus that most interested me: the leftist political movement and the art scene. Macario Matus now called me a person "*de confianza*" (to be trusted) and a prominent COCEI activist called me a "*ñero*" ("*compañero*," comrade or "bro"). Moreover, from that point on informants frequently visited me. I no longer had to constantly seek them out and twist their arms until they talked.

The party was gratifying also because it was a family affair: the Ruiz family (including myself) hosted visiting dignitaries from Juchitán. Even though life among my Zapotec in-laws was sometimes frustrating, while I lived in the Ruiz household in San Blas I always felt connected. I was always part of a larger unit, not just an isolated individual. The local people viewed me as an insider, which was an invaluable boon to my research. My domestic situation also provided a sense of emotional well-being that far outweighed any research advantages it conveyed. This was especially important given the stressful nature of fieldwork on radical politics.

At the end of a long day of interviews and field observations, or whenever I felt bored or confused, I could always hang out on our front sidewalk and socialize with family members, neighbors, and passersby. In the Isthmus, unlike at home in the United States, I was an uncle, brother-in-law, son-in-law, and so on; I had multiple kinship roles that gave me status and satisfaction. If I was thirsty and needed a beer, I could send my nephew Robertito down to the corner cantina for an ice-cold *caguama*.[1] Octavio, my brother-in-law, was always available to fix my old car or chat about baseball games or town gossip. In turn, my relatives looked to me for frequent favors and constant companionship.

As a child, my family was wracked by divorce. Today, though my U.S. relatives care about each other, like many Americans they live far apart in separate states and seldom have face-to-face contact. In the womb-like comfort of a San Blas family, I learned that tightly knit Oaxacan families and towns, far from being an anachronism, filled a deep human need for warmth and togetherness. I sincerely hope that the rapid economic "development" of the Isthmus will not ravage Zapotec home and community life the way it has devastated the physical environment. As my fieldwork came to a close, I realized how much I would miss my in-laws when I returned to the United States. At the birthday party I felt great pleasure at temporarily bringing together my Zapotec extended family with my research "subjects"/friends, the Juchiteco intellectuals and politicians.

I left the field in July 1988 just prior to the Mexican presidential elections. By then I felt that I had collected most of the material I needed to write my dissertation. Despite my enjoyment of the comforts of Zapotec domestic and social life, I was homesick for life in the United States. I departed San Blas in the station wagon in the middle of the night of July 12 (election day) along with my father-in-law and a Guatemalan friend, Chalo, and all of my notes from more than a year of fieldwork. I recklessly carried my computer and disks without leaving behind any back-up of research materials. It was also a dangerous move to drive at night on the Trans-Isthmus highway, which is infamous for the armed bandits who hold up buses and cars, especially in the stretch of road around Palomares, just past Juchitán. At the time, however, it seemed like the thing to do. In the adventurous spirit of my fieldwork, we hit the road.

The sweet nocturnal smells of the Chimalapas jungle heightened the sense of romantic adventure as we cruised toward Veracruz. As I think back on the experience, I am reminded of the comments of my Mexican friends who often chided me for my gringo caution and excessive meticulousness. Their philosophy was to take life head on, without regrets, with a dash of masculine zest (a concept deplored by U.S. academics as unforgiveable machismo). Some of this thinking, fortunately, had started to rub off on me.

En route we arrived at San Andrés Tuxtla, Veracruz, a pro-Cárdenas (leftist) town. The highway through San Andrés was blocked by Cardenista truck drivers who had parked their trucks sideways across the road in a protest against PRI vote fraud in favor of the *priísta* candidate Carlos Salinas de Gortari.[2] I entered a small police station to clarify the situation and the surly policeman at the desk refused to explain to me what the demonstration was about nor when we could get through. Unable to continue, we took dark back streets past the main plaza where Cardenista protesters were engaged in an angry demonstration against PRI vote fraud. The atmosphere was chaotic and surreal: a loud, noisy mob shouting anti-government slogans in the plaza at three in the morning, the election results unannounced and mysterious, the possibility of a national Cardenista insurrection in the air.

We were quickly accosted by a *madrina*.[3] The *madrina* signaled us to pull over onto a secluded side street. He accused us of going the wrong way on a one-way street and threatened us with trouble if we did not pay him a bribe. This all happened too fast for me to get scared. Fortunately, there were three of us and only one of him. Chalo boldly claimed to be a highway patrolman (*federal de caminos*). Outnumbered and outwitted, the *madrina* was forced to let us go.

In retrospect, I see the tremendous, unnecessary risks I took on this trip. I could easily have lost all of my hard-earned research notes. Yet I experienced so many challenging moments during my fieldwork—being threatened in bars, being hassled by customs agents on the Guatemala–Mexico border, wondering if I was being followed by government or leftist agents, struggling to gain interviews with suspicious political leaders, getting flat tires on dark roads late at night—that I began to gain a greater sense of trust in myself. I knew that I could survive such difficulties. Through my fieldwork, I also saw how poor Oaxacan families facing much more serious obstacles (bad health, few resources and many mouths to feed, unemployment, and political powerlessness) nonetheless confronted their problems with panache and gusto. Fieldwork, for me, was a kind of coming-of-age that had been delayed by years immersed in the University of Wisconsin library and the fervid, stifling air of graduate seminars.

Thankfully, the rest of the trip on the Mexican side of the border was uneventful, except for a flat tire, a broken muffler, and an overheated radiator. These automotive troubles were conveniently solved by my brother-in-law, Arturo, who runs a welding and mechanics shop in Piedras Negras, Veracruz. As soon as the car began to falter we headed toward Arturo's house and the Zapotec kinship network once again proved its value. After dropping off my father-in-law in Veracruz, we finally reached the border at Matamoros, Tamaulipas. I left Chalo at the border so that he could hire a *coyote* to take him to "the other side." At the U.S border crossing, I endured rude questions about what I was doing in Oaxaca and the indignity of a thorough search of my papers by a U.S. immigration official, but I was home and I heaved a sigh of relief at having made it to my home country with my precious fieldnotes, documents, and computer intact. I quickly went to a hotel in Brownsville, Texas, where Chalo was already waiting.

Unfortunately, because of the U.S. Immigration and Naturalization Service checkpoint on the highway north from Brownsville, I was forced to leave Chalo at a refugee center for undocumented Central Americans. I gave him fifty dollars and a big hug, but felt like a traitor. Chalo had accompanied me on some of my wildest times in the Isthmus cantinas and on a trip to Guatemala (made necessary by the expiration of my visa and car permit for travel in Mexico). I had met his entire family and they introduced me to the grandeur and horror of Guatemala, a beautiful country still recovering from a genocidal civil war. Chalo had become a steadfast friend to whom I owed many favors, but I really had no choice but to leave him in Texas (if I had taken him through the checkpoint he might have been deported to Guatemala). Eventually, Chalo made his way to San Antonio and through relentless, hard work established his own landscaping business, learned English, and started a family—a true immigrant success story.

The rest of the trip to Madison went by in a blur. I drove thirty-two hours straight to Wisconsin, anxious to reunite with my spouse, deliver my research materials to my house intact, and recuperate from recurrent stomach problems contracted in rural Mexico and the tensions of studying a radical political movement. As I parked the car in the driveway in Madison, I heaved another great sigh of relief. Except for a steady oil leak, my 1977 Malibu wagon had held up pretty well for a vehicle with 130,000 miles on the odometer. The car had suffered a broken speedometer cable, frayed fan belts, worn-out power steering hoses, leaky radiator hoses, flat tires, and miscellaneous other ailments, but thanks to my brother-in-law's patient care, it still looked sharp and ran smoothly.

My health was also fine other than a few minor problems. A medical check-up indicated that I had acquired several non-pathogenic parasites, stomach irritation from contaminated food and water, and dehydration. I also contracted a bad viral infection on my feet from wearing cheap Oaxacan huaraches which are cured with cattle dung and held together with nails. Over time the nails wore through the rubber soles and injured my feet, creating a vector for the infection to spread. Eventually, I had to have foot surgery to correct the growths created by the virus. But, considering the risks I had been exposed to, these ailments were relatively inconsequential.

Back in Wisconsin, I luxuriated in the comfort and convenience of life in the midwestern United States, as compared to rural Southern Mexico, but I soon became disillusioned by the extremely cold winters and the workaholic academic atmosphere of Madison. I had returned from the most exciting experience of my life in a warm, tropical place (the Isthmus), where as a visiting anthropologist and member of a local clan I had high social status. Now I was just another graduate student drone clutching my books under my coat to protect them from the Wisconsin snow as I trudged to the library.

It was a strange, uncanny feeling to have one's heart and soul focused on the tropics and one's body in the frozen north. This dissonance was also intellectually challenging. Though it might encourage a person to romanticize the greener grass "on the other side," deeper thinking made me realize that when I was in Oaxaca, I often longed for the convenience, efficiency, and modernity of U.S. life, while in the United States I missed the passion, traditions, and friendliness of Oaxaca. In the best spirit of cultural relativism, I tried to recognize the strengths and weaknesses of each cultural locale. Furthermore, distance from my fieldsite allowed me to step outside the flow of daily happenings and gain analytical perspective on the people and events of the Isthmus.

If my return to U.S. academic life and the chilly midwest was sometimes disappointing, the sheer pleasure of writing a thesis, relatively uninterrupted for a year, made up for it. I especially enjoyed reflecting on my experiences and the people I met and converting them to words and paragraphs on clean white computer paper, freshly laser-printed.

While writing the thesis I also was given the opportunity to coedit *Zapotec Struggles* (1993) and to publish an extensive body of work by my Juchiteco friends. This further established my reputation in Oaxaca and with my Zapotec intellectual friends. On future visits to Juchitán, people were much more anxious to talk with me than they were before publication of the book. Unfortunately, this mostly positive enterprise was marred by a conflict over the editorship of the volume. This bittersweet experience, however, taught me an important lesson about the commodification of anthropological knowledge and the ways in which anthropologists use ethnographic information to make their careers and livelihood. I had realized that, in the academy, anthropologists transformed rich, intensely personal fieldwork experiences (and idealistic graduate student goals) into scholarly books and articles that must compete in a divisive, commercialized market. I also quickly learned that journalists and filmmakers were interested in anthropological data, although some considered anthropologists to be just informants or resources rather than colleagues or collaborators. This made me realize even more how much anthropologists need to be careful to avoid exploiting the people we study (our informants).

As I began to publish, and after I obtained my first teaching job, I started to reap the fruits of my fieldwork: a small amount of recognition and prestige, although this was also accompanied by the usual academic ups and downs, alliances and conflicts. During my first year of teaching at UTEP, fresh out of graduate school and still full of idealism and innocence, I frequently wore my old fieldwork huaraches and *guayaberas* to class. I even had my students call me by my first name until I realized that they all seemed to want to call me "Doctor," which better fit their conception of a professor. Eventually I discarded the fieldwork garb; but I made my early reputation at UTEP through lectures about my research and a Oaxaca cultural performance and art exhibit I organized at the university museum. With a good salary and a home, I was able to invite many of my Juchiteco intellectual friends to stay with me. I was also able to use my academic connections to sell their paintings and publish their writings.

My main fieldwork period occurred between May 1987 and July 1988, but I continued to return to the Isthmus each summer and during some Christmas vacations. Additionally, I arranged to have Manuel Matus, a leading Zapotec writer and COCEI activist, live at my house and study for a master's degree at UTEP. At that point I felt I had come full circle; a "native key informant" lived in my house who could clarify

any point about COCEI or the Zapotec cultural movement over breakfast. As my friendship with Manuel and other Zapotec intellectuals
grew, I realized that I was no longer very interested in the traditional
ethnographer–informant relationship. Nor did I want to continue to
study radical politics—with its combination of high anxiety and adren-
aline rush excitement. I felt that my future work with Zapotecs should
be strictly collaborative, working (or simply being) with them as friends
rather than research subjects.

Ironically, my growing recognition in Juchitán and the United
States as a scholar of Oaxaca coincided with increasing distance from
my fieldsite. In December 1994 Obdulia and I adopted her sister's
daughter, Ruth. Ruth was born prematurely and suffered initially from
the Isthmus heat. Her health was shaky and we were unable to adopt
her in Mexico despite numerous attempts to do so (including several
bribes) with a local judge. Finally, we decided to return to El Paso with
Ruth, without adoption papers, to safeguard her health. We flew to
Mexico City and then Ciudad Juárez with our one-month old, undocumented child; the whole time we were afraid that someone would ask
us for her papers.

Ruth was morally ours. Her biological mother, Obdulia's sister
Margarita, had given us Ruth (her only female child) in a profound gesture of familial solidarity. Yet we lacked the thin piece of stamped, official paper that made her ours in the eyes of the government. Far more
than any other experience, this made me deeply sympathetic toward
the millions of undocumented Mexican people who struggle daily to
live their lives in peace in the belly of the U.S. beast.

In Juárez, we got a hotel room by the border and tried to figure out
what to do. After several days of anxious waiting we finally drove to El
Paso with Ruth in the backseat. Our immigration lawyer later said this
was a legal entry because we had not been asked and did not tell. In any
case, we eventually arranged for Ruth's adoption and immigration papers. My Zapotec daughter became a U.S. citizen. Another irony: I,
the anthropologist, had taken my child away from her native culture
and made her an "American."

Because Ruth had entered the U.S. under special circumstances, our
lawyer advised us not to take her out of the country until she obtained
her citizenship. Thus, for the first few years, our ability to travel back to
Oaxaca, the place I loved so dearly, was limited. My close connections
to Juchitán and the Isthmus also loosened when my marriage to
Obdulia began to unravel. One reason for the decline of the marriage

was the hedonistic lifestyle I had picked up in the Isthmus. The marriage dissolved amid great emotional pain, and I found myself wondering what had become of my relationship to the Isthmus Zapotec people now that I was no longer married to a local woman.

In addition to the loss of a spouse, I felt keenly the loss of a whole kinship network. In the United States, divorce may consist of no more than the end of a marriage contract between two people. Family and relatives may have no involvement and be unaffected by the process. In this case, my relationships with at least fifty in-laws were damaged and my valuable identity—for research purposes—as a member of a local family was gone.

From 1995 to 1999 I did not return to the Isthmus, although I spent considerable time with Juchiteco friends in Mexico City. My Zapotec friends assured me that despite the divorce I am still welcome in Juchitán. Yet it seemed best to stay away, at least for a while. I know, however, that I will always have a strong passion for the Isthmus of Tehuantepec and its people.

Does an anthropologist have a unique relationship to the group of people he or she studies? Does the intensity of the fieldwork experience forge bonds that are any different from those developed through normal friendships? Are fieldwork connections long lasting or strictly contingent and pragmatic? These isssues were put to the test in my own life and career in the aftermath of my divorce. My prolonged absence from the Isthmus and modified relationship to local people made me question the effects of time and distance on the deep ties of affinity and cooperation generated by fieldwork.

One cannot proffer answers to these questions for anyone but himself. It is my view, however, that the relationships developed in fieldwork (in spite of personal travails) do have a deep, almost sacred, meaning, at least to the anthropologist. Our informants may forget us but we will never forget them. Our professional, moral, and ethical commitment to informants and the cultures we study never ends. The obligation to write about people and cultures in ways that are life enhancing and not damaging to the subjects of study must be our fundamental principle. Without it we are lost. No amount of postmodern irony, glib discussions of "complicity," or allusions to the breakdown of identities by globalization can take the place of our basic commitment to protect the safety and well-being of those we write about.

This book has followed the postmodern agenda regarding the need for multisited research, although the primary fieldwork site was

Juchitán, Oaxaca. Recognizing the need for fieldwork in multiple places, I have engaged in ongoing dialogues with Zapotec people in various parts of Oaxaca and the United States, and even conducted a fascinating interview with a Zapotec woman in Belgium. Nowadays, I also communicate with Zapotec colleagues through the Internet as well as fax and telephone. Such an expansion of the traditional single locale methodology, however, should not be taken as a license to do shallow, jet-setting fieldwork. Anthropology should not be reduced to a kind of vulgar journalism. "Thick description" through long-term, deep immersion in one or more places and/or groups of people must remain our hallmark. The danger of the postmodernist call for multiple sites is the dilution of quality fieldwork in pursuit of quantity of shifting locations.

Despite these concerns, I have also found value in postmodern critiques of the naïve anthropologist/informant rapport; but rather than replace rapport with "complicity," I have emphasized collaboration. Anthropologists no longer "have" "their people"; this kind of paternalism is a thing of the past. Yet we still have close relationships with our "informants." These relationships compel anthropologists not only to protect the integrity and confidentiality of those they study, but also to contribute positively to the societies studied. I found that collaboration was the most viable way to do this.

Collaboration, of course, may not be possible or desirable for all ethnographers, especially those who study right-wing political movements, criminal subcultures, or other groups to which the anthropologist is philosophically opposed. In my research, I felt that collaboration through donations, joint publications, and cooperation on various cultural projects strengthened my ties with Isthmus people, benefitted local people's careers, and satisfied my desire to reciprocate for all the help given me by Zapotec people. I invite Marcus or other postmodern critics of the rapport concept to show how such collaboration is detrimental to "informants" or anthropology.

Although I concur with postmodern theorists on the need for ethnography that comes to grips with globalism and the "postmodern" phase of culture, I have chosen to continue anthropology's focus on the resistance struggles of "subaltern" people. Avoiding postmodern irony and moral neutrality, I have aligned my research with a social movement (COCEI) that I have defended in my writing and lectures. This is not to say that I have naïvely accepted all aspects of the movement or parroted its views. In fact, I have reported on COCEI corruption, internal conflicts, and tactical errors made by the *coceístas*. But I feel the positive impact of COCEI far outweighs its mistakes; my position is that anthropologists must take a political stand to defend endangered minority indigenous cultures, such as the Isthmus Zapotecs.

This ethnography was rooted in passionate commitment to particular people and a place (the Isthmus) because such personal and political ties are critical to a progressive politics that defends cultural survival, ecological well-being, and indigenous self-determination. The emotional element of political activism is especially important for academics, such as anthropologists, because we are far too prone to ivory tower debates in the classroom, at conferences, or on the pages of professional journals. These abstract discussions, however well-intentioned, may help elucidate arcane aspects of neo-Marxist or post-structuralist theory, but they do little for the people on the ground who are our research subjects. The passionate, politicized approach I advocate is not foolproof: relationships, collaborations, or marriages (as in this case) can break down. But I consider the benefits of advocacy and collaborative ethnography worth the risks.

I have also been critical of "political correctness" in anthropology, especially as I experienced it as a graduate student. Political correctness creates a dogmatic, formulaic view of the world that destroys the anthropological project of documenting and presenting the "messy" (i.e., not clear-cut, not easily reduced to simple slogans) lives of people in particular times and places. Many of my key informants were definitely not politically correct, but they were some of the most vibrant human beings I have ever met and they taught me many valuable lessons. Political correctness is also damaging to anthropology because it fetishizes certain words, such as "essentialism," "hegemony," and "transgression," that homogenize complex social realities and take the place of serious analysis.

I would like to close this account by discussing my Zapotec daughter Ruth's future in the transcultural postmodern world. Will she value her indigenous traditions, language, and land? Will she become a bilingual, Mexican American border person? Will she leave the Isthmus and Zapotec culture behind as she joins the frenetic pace of U.S. culture?

Though born in Oaxaca, Ruth has lived in the United States since she was one month old. Like most American children, my daughter is fond of Disney cartoons, Barbie dolls, and Pokémon. Ruth's primary language is English, which Obdulia insisted on speaking in the home to prevent Ruth from suffering the stigma she experienced as a nonnative speaker. Though phenotypically "Mexican," Ruth is for all intents and purposes an all-American girl. Her knowledge of Oaxaca is limited to a one-week vacation in the Isthmus. When she returned from the trip I asked her about what she learned in Mexico and the first thing she mentioned was how much she enjoyed playing Star Wars Episode I with her biological brother Max. She did not consider Oaxaca a radically separate and different world from her own in El Paso. What does this say about cultural processes in the global village?

Ruth's case is complicated by her residence in a predominantly Hispanic border community. El Paso/Ciudad Juárez is probably the most united and integrated of all U.S.–Mexican border towns. Connections and interactions between the two cities are ubiquitous and constant. In this context, Ruth is already gradually learning about Mexican culture from her mother, friends, and the larger urban community. She will eventually become fluent in Spanish and in many respects be bicultural, a Mexican American. But "Chicana" is a label her mother, who identifies first and foremost as Zapotec and secondly as a Mexican, roundly rejects. We both want to teach Ruth Zapotec culture, heritage, and language. Presumably she will also desire this as she gets older. But will it be possible, and how?

Discussions of globalism (or globalization) and its effects often raise the specter of cultural imperialism, of the hegemonic force of McDonalds, Toys "R" Us, television, malls, and so on, and the seductive power of U.S. lifestyles and products (see Ritzer 1999). My daughter is growing up in such a world and is fascinated by video movies and the endless toys and gadgetry available to American children. The U.S. middle-class consumer pattern is so strong that sometimes there seems little chance of resistance or cultural alternatives. But I retain hope that small-scale, indigenous cultures, like the Zapotecs, can survive and prosper in the new millennium. This will only be possible with tremendous effort on the part of individuals (especially parents, like myself, who must teach their children languages and customs) and organized groups like COCEI who must fight to defend their identities and traditions.

In northern Mexico, particularly Chihuahua, which borders El Paso, Indians and native culture are not highly valued. Many Chihuahuans view themselves as white descendants of Spaniards and other Europeans. To the extent that Indian background is recognized at all, it is not usually as a source of great pride. Southern Mexicans, such as those from Oaxaca and Veracruz, are often looked down upon as racially inferior indigenes. These same sentiments are common in El Paso and many local Mexican Americans pride themselves on speaking little Spanish and being highly assimilated to Anglo-American culture.[4] U.S genocidal treatment of American Indians is well known. In this context, Ruth's path toward reunification with her Zapotec heritage is fraught with obstacles.

Yet if her parents are determined enough, and if she has sufficient desire to learn about Oaxaca, then in the future, in spite of the homogenizing aspects of globalization, she may be able to steep herself in Zapotec ways. This will require, above all, exposure and contact with the Isthmus and its people: "being there," to invoke Geertz's celebrated phrase in a different context (Geertz 1988). In this sense, Ruth has an advantage: the vast Ruiz family kinship network. She has an Isthmus family eagerly awaiting her return and involvement in local life. But she has to want this herself, something that her parent's encouragement can perhaps enable. The media and cyberspace tools of the global era make it much easier for the curious to explore, albeit from a distance, the cultures of any part of the globe, and travel to Oaxaca from the United States is much simpler than when I first started my fieldwork. My own writings on Oaxaca may be an inspiration to my daughter. But all of these cultural decisions are ultimately Ruth's, and such decisions and challenges will shape the future for Isthmus Zapotec people.

NOTES

1. Quart-sized bottle.

2. In fact, PRI did commit fraud in order to prevent Cárdenas from winning and to install Carlos Salinas as president.

3. *Madrinas*, unofficial assistants to policemen, have a well-deserved reputation for corruption.

4. An exception to this are some Chicano activists who glorify an Indian past; however, this "Indian" past is usually conceived as Aztec, not Zapotec.

Epilogue

In May 2000, I finally returned to Juchitán as part of a human-rights delegation (sponsored by the San Francisco-based organization Global Exchange) to observe conditions prior to the July presidential elections. As I arrived in Mexico, I felt profoundly ambivalent. No longer the young adventurer married to a local woman and enthralled with an idealistic radical Indian movement, what was my role here? Was I just an "expert" passing through to gather "data" and share that wisdom with my North American colleagues? Or are all of my years in Oaxaca, decades thinking and dreaming about Oaxaca, loving Oaxaca and its people, worth something more, do they have some meaning?

Searching for answers, I could not wait to reach the Isthmus. While in Mexico City en route to Oaxaca, I began to feel seriously ill. I had been a bit under the weather prior to my departure from El Paso, but had delayed seeing a physician due to my impatience to get to Juchitán. My condition finally got so bad that, feverish and exhausted, I contacted a Mexican doctor through the hotel. His cure turned out to be worse than the original health problem.

The doctor diagnosed me with typhoid (which was highly unlikely) and gave me a penicillin shot in the buttocks followed by antibiotics and anti-fever medicine. I also took a sleeping pill in order to get some rest. But it was a terrible night. Not a wink of sleep. In the morning I was seeing double and was extremely tired. My balance was poor. I think this was mainly from taking too much antibiotic (the 400 mg. of Oranol prescribed by the doctor instead of the normal dose of 200 mg.).

Despite my pathetic condition I joined my fellow human-rights delegates at the Mexico City airport. In the airport I saw another doctor but he could find nothing wrong with me. We flew to Huatulco, Oaxaca, a luxurious tourist resort developed in the 1980s. I felt the irony of returning to my main field site in comfort (with money, staying at nice hotels), yet not feeling well enough to enjoy it. On the plane to Huatulco I tried to rest but could not sleep. My vision was extremely limited and I felt awful.

We arrived in Huatulco at 3:00 P.M., after a one-hour flight from Mexico City. There were few passengers on the flight, little tourism. As I discovered later, a Oaxacan guerrilla group called the EPR (*Ejército Popular Revolucionario*, People's Revolutionary Army) had attacked the Huatulco police station in 1996 and killed eleven people. Subsequently, international, and even domestic, tourism to Huatulco was drastically reduced. It was fiery hot and sunny in Huatulco. The airport employees and taxi drivers were stout, jovial Zapotec men. Even though I felt wretched, I was back in my fieldwork environment.

We took a taxi to the Hotel Binniguenda (named after mythical goblin-like creatures from Zapotec folklore). The vegetation along the road was the familiar dry, spiny coastal plants and trees. There were dogs lying on the road and poor people waiting at a crossroads for a bus to a small pueblo. We went into the tourist zone of Santa Cruz. Zapotec women were calmly walking through the streets wearing colorful dresses and plastic flip-flops. Their long, black hair hung down their backs. There were only a few gringo tourists.

The Hotel Binniguenda was decorated with Oaxacan red tile roofs and big tile floors that exuded a cool, earthy smell. There were large paintings by Oaxacan painters on the walls of the lounge area and restaurant, and the hotel was designed to have a Zapotec feel to it. One painting depicted the mysterious *binniguenda* creatures; alongside it on the wall hung a description of Oaxacan folklore by Andres Henestrosa. The hotel had a bar called Binniza (Zapotec people). The restaurant adjacent to it was called Guendaró (the Zapotec word for "food"). The dining area was tastefully adorned and emphasized tropical Oaxacan vegetation. The restaurant had high-pitched roofs with wooden beams and high ceilings. It had an open, airy feeling like that of traditional Isthmus homes. There was a decoration of stuffed and ceramic coastal animals on the wall, including an armadillo, and a green stone fountain reminiscent of the streets of Oaxaca City. As I enjoyed the comfortable surroundings, I could not help wondering if this was the future of Zapotec culture: to become the trappings for upscale tourist hotels.

It was muggy and I sweated copiously under the restaurant's wobbly electric fans. I had an excellent meal of fried red snapper and an orange chile sauce. After dinner I walked through the artificial tourist streets of Huatulco and through the beautiful plaza and park down to a nice waterfront park area. Local people were playing gently on the beach. A pretty open-air church overlooked the ocean. Istmeñas were selling food from plastic tubs. There were only a few tourists enjoying this paradisical setting. The EPR attack, though damaging to the local economy, had at least returned part of Oaxaca to the Oaxacans.

After a long fitful night I finally dozed off. I awoke at two in the morning unsure of where I was or what I was doing. I fell back to sleep and woke again at five in the morning. As I became conscious I realized that I was calling out "Ruthie, Ruthie" (my daughter's name). This is a recurrent nightmare I have that is related to my divorce and my no longer living with my daughter. On the trip, the issue of my relationship to Obdulia, Ruth, and Oaxacan peoples weighed heavily on my mind. I suppose this is what I hoped to clarify by coming to Mexico. Perhaps working through this would give me new insight into anthropology and myself.

We left Huatulco in a chauffered Suburban at 7:00 A.M. (May 24, 2000). It was warm and cloudy, rain fell sporadically throughout the drive. The coastal drive was gorgeous, unmarred by commercial signs and advertising. The driver even saw two toucans flying in the trees. The white flowers of the *cacahuastla*[1] trees and the stringy bushes were beautifully etched against the dense green vegetation, a product of the recent rains. The landscape was as fertile as I had ever seen it. The air was fresh and clean. It was the best of coastal Oaxaca: spectacular, primitive beaches; high mountain vistas of wide ocean; broad, luxuriant valleys of rich volcanic soil; tiny Indian towns with unique traditions (Santiago Astata, Morro Mazatán, Rincón Bamba).

The driver explained that the EPR attack on Huatulco in 1996 had nearly destroyed local commerce and permanently cancelled a regular Continental Airlines flight from Houston. He repeated a version of events in which the perpetrators of the attack were paid 2,000 pesos for doing it, and he said it must have been outsiders because local people cannot afford guns. He said there was a conspiracy in the Mexican press to report only bad news about Huatulco. Listening to these convoluted stories, I felt back in my element: the murky world of Oaxacan political intrigue.

On the way to Salina Cruz we crossed only one military checkpoint—the normal one near the salt flats, close to town. We were waved through without having to show our passports. We saw little military presence in Huatulco or on the road. Apparently, the driver's apocalyptic vision and reports I had received in the United States about the militarization of Oaxaca were exaggerated. I noticed that the outskirts of Salina Cruz on the way to Tehuantepec had expanded dramatically. There were new businesses, housing complexes, government buildings, and single-family homes everywhere. Little could be seen of the rural Zapotec peasant culture. The only representation of Zapotec life to be found was on the walls of restaurants boasting of regional cuisine. It seemed that one of my worst fears was coming to fruition: the destruction of Isthmus indigenous culture by rampant Western-style development.

Riding in the Suburban, I felt like a tourist passing through, seeing everything from a distance through glass windows, with no connection to the local people. I also felt like a villain, avoiding being seen by ex-in-laws. In Tehuantepec we ate breakfast at the Restaurant Guieshoba.[2] In the window by the entrance were Tehuana dolls in plastic containers, symbolic of the artificial use of local culture to promote the restaurant.

On the highway to Juchitán we saw few billboards. This may be the result of devastation wrought by Hurricane Paulina that hit the region in 1998. In any case, the road was rebuilt. It was flat, solid, and wide. There was still abundant agricultural land and wild scrublands between Tehuantepec and Juchitán, unlike the area between Tehuantepec and Salina Cruz. This preservation of communal and *ejido* land and defense of farmer's rights is a COCEI accomplishment. There was very little commercial development on either side of the road. Beauty and ecology have been preserved—thanks, in part, to COCEI.

Juchitán was booming and busy as always. We arrived and got rooms at La Mansión hotel. The other members of my group left for Matías Romero to conduct interviews and I stayed in Juchitán to try to recover my eyesight and arrange contacts with COCEI. I called my first major Juchiteco informant, Manuel López Mateos, and he warmly invited me to a fiesta. I declined because of my eye problems and arranged to meet with him the next morning at his home. Apparently, any tension there had been between us was now gone.

Concerned about my health, I called a local physician to try to determine what was wrong with my eyes. He affirmed what I suspected: excess antibiotic can cause double vision. I decided to quit taking the antibiotic. But my vision did not improve and I could not rest. Since my eyesight was not improving I called an eye doctor. It turned out that Arthur Hayton, an expatriate American doctor, was still in the phone book, and he was in when I called. Hayton vaguely remembered me and agreed to see me right away. I decided to walk to his office because the streets were clogged with cars and people that formed the procession of the *Vela San Isidro*. I could only see out of my right eye, and with both eyes open saw blurry or double. I stumbled across the street in front of La Mansión and tried to make my way to Dr. Hayton's office. I reeled and staggered through the muddy, rock-strewn Juchitán streets like a drunk.

The trip became a nightmare, an odyssey of fear heightened by the extreme heat and humidity. There were too many obstacles: potholes, piles of rubble, people walking everywhere, men on horseback, the endless fiesta procession, rain, and bottle rockets going off and startling me. It was Boschian chaos. I had to walk far out of my way to avoid the procession. I went down dead-end alleys. Drunks gave me misleading directions. I was afraid I would be mugged. Men on horses came up rapidly behind me. I was overwhelmed with anxiety. Ironically, my path to a Western medical cure for my eye problems had been blocked by the Zapotec revellers of a traditional fiesta.

On any other occasion, I would have been one of the celebrants, an anthropologist engaged in participant observation. But this time I did not want to be seen by Juchiteco friends—this would only delay my arrival and cause more stress. I asked directions of burly policemen and soldiers carrying heavy rifles. I got wrong directions, took wrong turns. Finally, I made it to Dr. Hayton's office.

Hayton seemed to recognize me although he also confused me at times with some other gringo who flew a Cessna 210 plane. He kept asking me about airplane engines. I was only concerned about what was wrong with my eyes. Because of my panic about my eyesight, everything seemed bizarre. The doctor slowly took me into his stuffy, airless office. The room was full of mechanical gadgets that in my state of anxiety I found threatening. It felt like a torture chamber. The doctor methodically checked my eyes with various gadgets. He said very little and asked few questions, which only increased my fears. I wondered if the old doctor, by now in his early eighties at least, still knew his business. I tried to explain to him that the problem was coming from too much antibiotics and that I could barely see. I thought my eyesight was ruined.

I felt like only the whites of my eyes were showing. I was in a state of sheer terror. He gave me several eye tests—all of which showed little vision in my left eye and blurriness when both eyes were used together. He said he could not see my optic nerve. The doctor forced my eyes open and put drops in them that burned. The doctor's comments were cryptic and confusing. He said I had a loose or torn eye muscle and that perhaps I had an infection that reduced my vision, or that maybe the antibiotic had caused it. His comments were ambiguous, although he said my eyes would be fine in about a month and a half.

Dr. Hayton began typing up his diagnosis on an old typewriter. He said I had a vitamin deficiency for which he prescribed B complex vitamins taken orally and by injection. At that point the last thing I wanted was another shot. I wanted instant relief from my eye problems and something to calm myself down. I told the doctor I could not see well enough to walk home and he did a few more tests but did not relieve my worries.

He finally concluded and typed up more prescriptions on the back of the original form. He added another antibiotic to the list. Another antibiotic? My biggest concern was that the previous dose of antibiotics had caused the problem in the first place and now he was prescribing new ones. There was still no resolution to my problems.

I was at my wit's end. Panic-stricken, for the first time in my life I felt like I had no idea what to do. I was immobilized by anxiety. I could not see and had no hope of immediate improvement. I asked the doctor if I could rest awhile. He said yes and took me upstairs to his living quarters. I felt like I was going to have a heart attack or stroke. The doctor said he did not believe in tranquilizers. He said that I should just relax and I would be better in a few hours. He said he would take me to the pharmacy to get the medication and shot and that would take care of my problems.

I lay in his hammock and drank five glasses of water but felt no relief. He offered little comfort. After about half an hour, I felt like there was nothing left to do but leave. I asked the doctor how much I owed him, just to get a response. He said I only owed him for the medicines he prescribed. The doctor offered no encouragement or support other than to say "we'll go get the other medicine from the pharmacy." I had no desire to leave his house but I had no choice.

I lumbered after the old man, covering my left eye so that I could find the way. It felt strange to be the young anthropologist gropingly following the elderly, expatriate doctor. So much for the hegemonic "seeing eye" of the Western anthropological gaze (Pratt 1992). All I wanted to do was see the sidewalk ten feet ahead of me, not cruelly misrepresent some native. At the pharmacy there was another ordeal. I had to go to a backroom to receive a vitamin shot in the buttocks. Finally we left and Dr. Hayton took me to a cab on 16 de Septiembre Street. I made it to the hotel safe and sound, although my vision was still bad.

At the hotel I tried to settle myself by contacting my wife and the rest of the group but no one was available. I rehydrated with large amounts of Gatorade but the anxiety remained. It subsided some when I told Steve Morris, a member of the Global Exhange delegation, what had happened. I called my wife and she broke down in tears when I told her about my problems. I felt better sharing the experience with others but I still felt like a failure as an anthropologist, human-rights observer, and traveller. How could this have happened to me, especially in the Isthmus where I did my research? I blamed myself when the problem was really an excessive dose of antibiotics. The experience reminded me of Artaud's bout of madness in the Sierra Tarahumara, Huxley eyeless in Gaza or southern Mexico, Burroughs and Kerouac wiped out by heroin in Mexico City, and the Consul's drunken delirium in *Under the Volcano*. Campbell loses it in Juchitán. But it happened and I had to deal with it.

What finally snapped me out of the worst of my depression was recounting the experience to Luis Matias Cruz, a member of the Global Exchange delegation who is originally from Oaxaca. As I told Luis what happened I periodically nodded off from exhaustion. He understood my problem and talked me through it. I explained to Luis that it was a *susto*-like experience.[3] He understood the concept from growing up in Oaxaca but encouraged me to break out of my negative mind-set through faith. He spoke to me of Christianity and religion. I felt receptive to this message but felt that if there was a god, that god would be a nonethnocentric god, perhaps a Zapotec god or a multicultural god, a god of peace and universality, not a racist god.

Luis gave me a vigorous, full-body massage and soothingly talked me through my anxieties. After an hour of this I felt much better. Eventually I dozed fitfully with frightful delusions and weird dreams until I finally slept soundly in the early hours of the morning. I awoke feeling much better and my vision was, remarkably, back to normal. Clearly, Luis' Oaxacan method was superior, in this case, to Dr. Hayton's Western medical approach.

Anxious to salvage my return trip to Juchitán, and resume my ethnographic work, I rushed to López Mateos's house. Rusty from too many years away from my fieldsite, I had trouble finding the way to Manuel's house, so I went to his mother-in-law's hardware store in downtown Juchitán. There was *Na* Manuela, now partially blind but gloriously powerful in her rustic old store, bossing around several teenage employees. Her hair was now white and her vision poor, but she still had the domineering spirit of a true Juchiteca business woman. *Na* Manuela held my hand and took me to the little entranceway into the alley that leads to the house. She did not remember me but I sure remembered her. She was a monument of strength, now perhaps ninety years old and still going strong.

The house was abundantly green and tropical. A large pistachio tree stood majestically in the yard. Libia, Manuel's wife, received me warmly with "Is that you Howard?" We hugged each other and then she took me to Manuel, who was waking up on a sofa in an anteroom. He had been drinking at the *Vela San Isidro* the night before until 4:30 in the morning. He had the same bald pate with Einstein-like flaps of fuzzy hair on each side of his head, a prominent nose, bare chest, and long thin legs. As usual he was not wearing a shirt, and he was jovial after a night of carousing. Manuel was looking well. Libia had some grey in her hair, but was still as pretty and fiery as ever.

We sat around the coffee table and talked about COCEI and the Isthmus Zapotec intellectuals over coffee and then beer. It was just like old times. Later we were joined by Desiderio de Gyves ("Deyo"), the current director of the Juchitán Cultural Center. I learned that years of COCEI control of Juchitán City Hall had led to problems of corruption and division within the COCEI ranks. Yet it seemed clear that the passion and vibrance of Zapotec culture in Juchitán were still alive and well in the twenty-first century, even if the grassroots political movement had lost much of its luster and idealism.

In the afternoon, we adjourned to a combination fish restaurant and cantina along the banks of the *Río de los Perros* that runs through Juchitán. On our way to the restaurant, we walked through a crowd of people, rows of empty wooden chairs, a bandstand, and dozens of broken bottles—visible signs of the previous night's fiesta that was preparing to resume. I felt at home in the grimy Juchitán streets and amid the rattling sounds and spicy aromas of Zapotec families eating lunch and going about their daily business. These were the familiar scenes of so many afternoons of fieldwork in the Isthmus.

At the restaurant/cantina we carried on our discussions of Juchiteco politics and culture while drinking frosty Coronas and succulent baked fish and crisp *totopos*. Manuel brought me up to date on the recent gossip about our Zapotec intellectual friends and COCEI politicians. Throughout the conversation we bantered with the proprietor in Spanish and Zapotec. Don José, the owner, joked that gringos had long penises. I countered that since I had recently divorced and his daughter was a widow, then we should get married immediately. The joking and the beer helped me get over the previous day's anxiety. I knew then that I could and would do more research in the Isthmus someday.

For nostalgia's sake I made a quick trip to the *Casa Verde* cantina. It was the same languid, decadent scene as always. As the rain fell, the mood in the bar was hot and erotic. At La Mansión I had one of the best meals I have ever eaten: a stunningly fresh, tender, and delicious *pulpo al mojo de ajo* (octopus fried in garlic).

Despite my eye problems, the return to Juchitán was a success. The 2000 Mexican presidential elections also turned out well. Vicente Fox, the candidate of the PAN (*Partido Acción Nacional*, National Action Party) upset the PRI's Francisco Labastida. This ended the PRI's seventy-one-year stranglehold on the Mexican government, and bodes well for opposition movements like COCEI. Its consequences for indigenous cultures are unclear, but the demise of PRI dominance is a source of satisfaction and hope for most Mexicans.

As I reflect on my experiences in Oaxaca, past and present, I realize that whatever problems occurred in my career and life as a result of my decision to do fieldwork in Juchitán (even the nightmarish eye difficulties), I will never regret it. It was the best time of my life; it gave me a sense of purpose and direction. In the future, I will continue to pursue collaborations with my Zapotec colleagues whenever possible—hopefully I can give back to them as much as they have given me.

NOTES

1. This spelling is from my original fieldnotes and is probably incorrect. I was unable to confirm the proper spelling of this word.

2. *Guieshoba*, or *guie xhuuba'*, are Zapotec words for jasmine, one of the most beautiful Isthmus flowering shrubs and an important element of local folklore.

3. *Susto* is a "folk" illness common in Mesoamerica in which a person who has gone through a frightening experience is deemed to be seriously ill. The normal cure for *susto* is a spiritual cleansing called a "*limpia*," which often includes a massage.

Bibliography

Ahmed, Akbar, and Cris Shore, eds. *The Future of Anthropology: Its Relevance to the Contemporary World*. London: Athlone Press, 1995.

Behar, Ruth. *Translated Woman: Crossing the Border with Esperanza's Story*. Boston: Beacon Press, 1993.

Best, Steven. *The Politics of Historical Vision: Marx, Foucault, Habermas*. New York: Guilford Press, 1995.

Best, Steven, and Douglas Kellner. *Postmodern Theory: Critical Interrogations*. New York: Guilford Press, 1991.

——— . *The Postmodern Turn*. New York: Guilford Press, 1997.

Bourgois, Phillipe. *In Search of Respect. Selling Crack in El Barrio*. Cambridge: Cambridge University Press, 1995.

Campbell, Howard. "Juchitán: The Politics of Cultural Revivalism in an Isthmus Zapotec Community." *Latin American Anthropology Review* 2 (1990): 47–55.

——— . "Tradition and the New Social Movements: The Politics of Isthmus Zapotec Culture." *Latin American Perspectives*, vol. 20, no. 3, issue 78 (1993): 83–97.

——— . *Zapotec Renaissance: Ethnic Politics and Cultural Revivalism in Southern Mexico*. Albuquerque: University of New Mexico Press, 1994.

——— , ed. *The Politics of Ethnicity in Southern Mexico*. Vanderbilt University Publications in Anthropology 50. Nashville, TN: Vanderbilt University, 1996.

Campbell, Howard, et al., eds. *Zapotec Struggles: Histories, Politics, and Representations from Juchitán, Oaxaca*. Washington, DC: Smithsonian Institution Press, 1993.

Campbell, Howard, and Susanne Green. "A History of Representations of Isthmus Zapotec Women." *Identities* 3, nos. 1–2 (1996): 155–82.

Clifford, James. *The Predicament of Culture: Twentieth-Century Ethnography, Literature, and Art*. Cambridge: Harvard University Press, 1988.

———. *Routes: Travel and Translation in the Late Twentieth Century*. Cambridge: Harvard University Press, 1997.

Clifford, James, and George Marcus, eds. *Writing Culture: The Poetics and Politics of Ethnography*. Berkeley: University of California Press, 1986.

Covarrubias, Miguel. *Mexico South*. New York: Alfred A. Knopf, 1946.

Cruz Martínez, Alejandro, et al. The *Woman Who Outshone the Sun: The Legend of Lucía Zenteno*. San Francisco: Children's Book Press, 1991.

Cummings, Michael. *Beyond Political Correctness: Social Transformation in the United States*. Boulder, CO: Lynne Rienner, 2000.

de la Cruz, Víctor, ed. *La Flor de la Palabra*. Mexico City: Premia Editora, 1983.

Fischer, Michael. "Worlding Cyberspace: Toward a Critical Ethnography in Time, Space, and Theory." In *Critical Anthropology Now: Unexpected Contexts, Shifting Constituencies, Changing Agendas*, edited by G. Marcus, 245–304. Santa Fe, NM: School of American Research Press, 1999.

Foster, George. "Treasure Tales, and the Image of the Static Economy in a Mexican Peasant Community." *Journal of American Folklore* 77 (1964): 39–44.

Geertz, Clifford. *Works and Lives. The Anthropologist as Author*. Stanford: Stanford University Press, 1988.

Gupta, Akhil, and James Ferguson, eds. *Anthropological Locations: Boundaries and Grounds of a Field Science*. Berkeley: University of California Press, 1997.

Gutmann, Matthew. *The Meanings of Macho: Being a Man in Mexico City*. Berkeley: University of California Press, 1996.

Henestrosa, Andrés. *Los Hombres Que Dispersó la Danza*. Mexico City: SEP, 1987.

———. "The Foundation of Juchitán." In *Zapotec Struggles: Histories, Politics, and Representations from Juchitán, Oaxaca*, edited by H. Campbell et al., 39–40. Washington, DC: Smithsonian Institution Press, 1993.

Hobsbawm, Eric, and Terence Ranger. *The Invention of Tradition*. Cambridge: Cambridge University Press, 1983.

Hubinger, Vaclav, ed. *Grasping the Changing World: Anthropological Concepts in the Postmodern Era*. New York: Routledge, 1996.

Lowry, Malcolm. *Under the Volcano*. Mithcham, Victoria, Australia: Penguin, 1962.

Marcus, George. *Ethnography Through Thick and Thin*. Princeton, NJ: Princeton University Press, 1998.

———. "Critical Anthropology Now: An Introduction." In *Critical Anthropology Now: Unexpected Contexts, Shifting Constituencies, Changing Agendas*, edited by G. Marcus, 3–28. Santa Fe, NM: School of American Research Press.

Matus, Macario. *La Noche de Tus Muslos*. Juchitán, Mexico: Casa de la Cultura de Juchitán, 1986.

———. *Poerótica*. Toluca, Mexico: Editorial La Tinta del Alcatraz, 1995.

Mintz, Sidney. "Sow's Ears and Silver Linings: A Backward Look at Ethnography." *Current Anthropology* 41, no. 2 (2000): 169–89.

Moore, Henrietta, ed. *The Future of Anthropological Knowledge*. New York: Routledge, 1996.

Neza. Mexico: Ediciones Toledo, 1987 (originally published 1935–1939).

Neza Cubi. Mexico: Talleres Gráficos de México, 1968–1970.

Ortner, Sherry. "Some Futures of Anthropology." *American Ethnologist* 26, no. 4 (1999): 984–991.

Ostler, Rosemarie. "Disappearing Languages." *The Futurist* 7, no. 6 (1999): 16–22.

Pratt, Mary Louise. *Imperial Eyes: Travel Writing and Transculturation*. New York: Routledge, 1992.

Rabinow, Paul. *Reflections on Fieldwork in Morocco*. Berkeley: University of California Press, 1977.

———. "Representations are Social Facts: Modernity and Post-Modernity in Anthropology." In *Writing Culture: The Poetics and Politics of Ethnography*, edited by J. Clifford and G. Marcus, 234–61. Berkeley: University of California Press, 1986.

Ritzer, George. *Enchanting a Disenchanted World. Revolutionizing the Means of Consumption*. Thousand Oaks, CA: Pine Forge Press, 1999.

Rosaldo, Renato. *Ilongot Headhunting, 1883–1974: A Study in Society and History*. Stanford, CA: Stanford University Press, 1980.

———. *Culture and Truth: The Remaking of Social Analysis*. Boston: Beacon Press, 1989.

Rubin, Jeffrey. *Decentering the Regime: Ethnicity, Radicalism and Democracy in Juchitán, Mexico*. Durham, NC: Duke University Press, 1997.

Ruiz Campbell, Obdulia. "Representations of Isthmus Women: A Zapotec Woman's Point of View." In *Zapotec Struggles: Histories, Politics, and Representations from Juchitán, Oaxaca*, edited by H. Campbell, 137–41. Washington, DC: Smithsonian Institution Press, 1993.

Tyler, Stephen. "Post-Modern Ethnography: From Document of the Occult to Occult Document." In *Writing Culture: The Poetics and Politics of Ethnography*, edited by J. Clifford and G. Marcus, 122–40. Berkeley: University of California Press, 1986.

——— . *The Unspeakable: Discourse, Dialogue, and Rhetoric in the Postmodern World*. Madison: University of Wisconsin Press, 1987.

Warren, Kay. *Indigenous Movements and Their Critics: Pan-Maya Activism in Guatemala*. Princeton, NJ: Princeton University Press, 1998.

Newspapers Cited

Unomásuno. Mexico City
Excelsior. Mexico City
Extra de Oaxaca. Oaxaca, Oaxaca
El Paso Times. El Paso, Texas

Index

About the Author

HOWARD CAMPBELL is Associate Professor of Anthropology, University of Texas-El Paso.